PHENOMENOLOGY

Northwestern University
Studies in Phenomenology
and
Existential Philosophy

Founding Editor **James M. Edie**

General Editors **John McCumber**
David Michael Levin

Consulting Editors

Robert Bernasconi
Judith P. Butler
David Carr
Edward S. Casey
Stanley Cavell
Roderick M. Chisholm
Hubert L. Dreyfus
Lester Embree
Dagfinn Føllesdal
Véronique Fóti
Irene Harvey
Dieter Henrich
Don Ihde
Emmanuel Levinas
Alphonso Lingis
William McBride

J. N. Mohanty
Maurice Natanson
Graeme Nicholson
Frederick Olafson
Paul Ricoeur
Tom Rockmore
George Schrader
Calvin O. Schrag
Thomas Sheehan
Hugh J. Silverman
Robert Sokolowski
Herbert Spiegelberg
Charles Taylor
Samuel J. Todes
Bruce W. Wilshire
David Wood

PHENOMENOLOGY

Between Essentialism and Transcendental Philosophy

J. N. Mohanty

Northwestern University Press
Evanston, Illinois

Northwestern University Press
625 Colfax
Evanston, Illinois 60208-4210

Copyright © 1997 by Northwestern University Press
All rights reserved
Printed in the United States of America

ISBN 0-8101-1401-1 cloth
    0-8101-1402-X paper

Library of Congress Cataloging-in-Publication Data

Mohanty, Jitendranath, 1928–
    Phenomenology : between essentialism and transcendental philosophy / J.N. Mohanty.
      p. cm.—(Northwestern University studies in phenomenology and existential philosophy)
    Collection of essays, some of which were previously published and some that are revised versions of the author's lectures given at the Univ. of Puerto Rico, Feb. 1991.
    Includes bibliographical references and index.
    ISBN 0-8101-1401-1 (cloth : alk. paper).—ISBN 0-8101-1402-X (paper : alk. paper)
    1. Phenomenology. 2. Phenomenology—History. I. Title.
II. Series: Northwestern University studies in phenomenology & existential philosophy.
B829.5.M632   1997
142'.7—dc21   097-6392
                                                                                        CIP

The paper used in this publication meets the minimum requirements of the American National Standard for Information Sciences—Permanence of Paper for Printed Library Materials, ANSI Z39.48–1984.

For

Jim Edie

in Friendship

Contents

Preface		xi
1	Themes and Tensions within Phenomenology	1
2	Max Scheler's Theory of Knowledge	14
3	Nicolai Hartmann's Phenomenological Ontology	25
4	Roman Ingarden's Critique of Husserl's Transcendental Phenomenology	32
5	Noema and Essence	46
6	Transcendental Philosophy and Lifeworld	52
7	On Derrida's Reading of Husserl	62
8	Foucault as a Philosopher	77
9	Phenomenology: Between Essentialism and Transcendental Philosophy	88
Notes		95
Index		103

Preface

The Background

There are many misunderstandings of phenomenology, each of which has been the basis of a certain line of criticism perpetuated over the years. Analytic philosophers find in phenomenology an unverifiable appeal to the privacy of one's experience, whereas in truth Husserlian phenomenology starts with an insistence upon the integral unity of language, thought, and experience. Many critics, dating back to the beginnings of phenomenology have found fault with the appeal to intuition, especially to the so called intuition of essences. In truth, this intuitionism, correctly understood, posits no special or extraordinary ability on the part of the phenomenologists, and amounts to no more than distinguishing, with regard to essences, between "empty" thinking and thinking backed by appropriate evidence. Suspicion of essences as a special sort of objects range from finding them inadmissible on the ground of a nominalistic preconception to finding them useless on the ground that they lack causal power. Husserl's essentialism was first challenged, from within phenomenology, by existential phenomenologists, then by various breeds of contemporary thinkers so much so that, like the term "Cartesian," the term "essentialist" was transformed from being a descriptive label to a pejorative one. Historicists eschewed essentialism, not realizing that only essences (and their kins, meanings) could have histories. Others, inspired by the universality of temporality and therefore of flux, found no place for essences—not realizing that there could be a genuine issue as to whether everything is temporal, and what is more, not seeing that to be temporal is not equivalent to being in flux (for, as Kant held, permanence is also a mode of being in time). To the dogmatism of intuitionism one contraposes the critical spirit of transcendental thinking, and one is puzzled by finding both together in phenomenology. Again one associated with transcendental philosophy a fixed grid of conceptual framework (such as the Kantian system of categories), and wondered how Husserl could both be a transcendental thinker and yet turn to a certain sort of historicism. Many of these criticisms arise from looking at a certain phase of Husserl's thinking exclusively. Looking at its totality, however, one begins to marvel at how things fall into place. Hopefully, the chapters to follow—which recall criticisms by his students and colleagues as well as by some of our contemporaries—will contribute to a more sympathetic appreciation of phenomenological philosophy.

Chapters 1 through 4 are revised versions of lectures originally given at the University of Puerto Rico in February of 1991. Chapter 5 was originally a commentary on a paper by Dagfinn Føllesdal and appeared in *The Phenomenology of the Noema,* ed. Drummond and Embree (Kluwer, 1992). Chapter 7 was written for Jim Edie and appears in a *Festschrift* for him: *Phenomenology and Skepticism: Essays in Honor of James M. Edie,* ed. Brice R. Wachterhauser (Northwestern, 1996). Chapter 8 appeared in *Foucault and the Critique of Institutions,* ed. Caputo and Yount (Penn State Press, 1993). Chapter 9 brings together the two themes "essence" and "constitution" around which these chapters revolve, as is indicated by the title. The chapter will show how this author understands Husserl's philosophy.

1

Themes and Tensions within Phenomenology

If one surveys the large range of philosophical concerns that characterize Husserl's writings, one can distinguish between several broad inquiries and theses focusing upon the following themes. Very schematically, these are: (1) essence, (2) meaning, (3) transcendental subjectivity, and (4) lifeworld. The particular order in which I have listed them might suggest—and that is not entirely mistaken—a certain chronological ordering of Husserl's concerns. But I do not for the present want to insist on the way Husserl's thinking developed.[1] I would rather draw attention to certain central themes of phenomenology, especially Husserl's, and to certain logical connections between them as also to certain perceived tensions. This exposition will provide me with the background for the chapters to follow.

Phenomenology started out with the program of describing essences and essential structures of various regions of phenomena. As a matter of fact, if one recalls the well-known slogan "*Zurück zu den Sachen selbst*," one may say, to begin with, that these *Sachen selbst* were regarded as *essences* and essential structures characterizing various regions. Let us not for the present worry about the concept of "region."[2] Examples of "region," in actual phenomenological research, are: "material nature," "human existence," "consciousness," "works of art," and "moral experience." Each of these regions is characterized not only by a highest regional essence, but also by a complicated essential structure, which the phenomenologists set out, in the spirit of scientific research, to uncover.

But by a curious transformation of that concern, phenomenology also began to perceive itself as being concerned with meanings, not merely with meanings of words and sentences, but also—by an extension of the concept of meaning—with meanings of experiences, of perceptions, beliefs, hopes and desires, *in fine*, of intentional acts. With this transformation, the concept of *noema* came to the focus of phenomenology.

1

Whereas the concept of essence was an ontological concept, an essence being an entity of a certain sort, an ideal entity to be sure, nevertheless an entity belonging to the world, the concept of meaning is a semantic concept to begin with but then, in the extended sense given to it by phenomenology, becomes ambiguously poised in between the mind and the world, being the way the world is presented to experience.

But it becomes immediately clear that a meaning is a correlate of an act of meaning, so that it is not the detached meaning, reified into an ideal, self-existent entity, but rather the correlation between an act and its meaning, between what in the jargon of the school was called *noesis* and its *noema*, which is the proper theme for phenomenological investigation. What is this correlation, but the very essence of consciousness, stripped of all naturalistic constructions? Thus, phenomenology finds its own domain for investigation: it is *consciousness*—construed not as natural phenomenon belonging to an entity that belongs to nature, but in its inmost essence as the correlation between noesis and noema, between the temporal act and the atemporal meaning.[3] From this, it needed a short step to be able to recognize that, as so construed, consciousness constitutes the world, confers sense on all things, not only provides access to the world, but is the very presenting of the world, making it evident, the source of its being and validity. Phenomenology becomes transcendental phenomenology.

One more step had to be taken by Husserl to radicalize even that claim to transcendentality. It would seem as though prior to all scientific thinking, prior to all theorizing—thus, prior to even philosophy as phenomenology—there is the world as lived by us in our everyday life, the world of perception and interest, valuations and actions, which has not yet been transformed by our thoughts and theories into the objective world amenable to scientific precision and theoretical idealization. Or, should philosophy just leave it behind as not being its proper subject matter? Should philosophy think about the world only as science presents it, thematizes it, measures it, conceptualizes it? It can do so, as Kantian thinking did, but only at the cost of denying its own claim to presuppositionlessness. How can it be the first science, if there is a first, pregiven ground which it cannot thematize, but which it must simply presuppose? Phenomenology, as transcendental philosophy, as philosophy which purports to uncover the foundation of all cognition, must recover this ground from its everyday anonymity. Husserl, therefore, turned to the lifeworld as the great theme for phenomenology.[4]

But if a science of the lifeworld is not to be empirical ethnology, if it is still to be philosophy, it has to uncover the essential structure of lifeworld, and not merely its contingent, variable features, features which vary from community to community. And it must also raise, even with regard to this lifeworld, the transcendental question as to the conditions of the possibility of a lifeworld. We shall have occasions to find out what such a question may after all mean. But for the present, we have completed the trajectory, in its barest outline, which Husserl's phenomenology followed. By following such a trajectory, phenomenology gave rise to questions as to its own internal consistency as well as regarding its viability as a philosophy. To some of these last questions, I will return at the end. Now I want to return to this very trajectory, and elaborate a little more the nature of these thematic concepts and the motivations for the transitions from one to the other.

Essence

First as to the essences. What are they, and why should phenomenology regard them as its proper subject matter?

There is no doubt that Husserl conceived of transcendental phenomenology as a science of essences as distinguished from sciences of facts: "a science which aims exclusively at establishing 'knowledge of essences' and *absolutely no 'facts.'* "[5] Why does he want phenomenology to be restricted to knowledge of essences alone?

I would distinguish between one ontological reason and another epistemological reason. The first consists in considerations arising out of Husserl's concern that all naturalism, including psychologism—as a matter of fact, all sorts of reductionism—need to be refuted, if philosophy is to be grounded on a sound basis. All such reductions are based on some science of fact or other—notably on psychology. A reduction of logic, for example, to psychology, is mistaken, because it distorts, and so is incompatible with, the very essence of the logical as such. A reduction of consciousness to states of the body likewise loses sight of the very essence of consciousness, i.e., its intentionality. A reduction of morality to social and psychological conditions would inevitably miss the very essence of morality, i.e., its "ought"-character. If the world of facts is carved up by the different sciences of fact into different regions as their domains, the very possibility of such sciences, in fact, their very legitimacy, would depend upon how those sciences presuppose the essential structures of the domains with which they are concerned. Thus, a distinction between fact and essence preserves the uniqueness of the domain from all reductionist attempts, and assigns the task of a philosophical explication of those essences to phenomenology and thus preserves the classical role of philosophy to provide the conceptual foundations for the sciences of fact.[6]

The epistemological reason for insisting on the essentialism of transcendental phenomenology is this: if phenomenology is to be a foundational *science*, its results must be necessary truths and not contingent ones. Of the real world of individuals, one cannot assert necessary truths, unless those truths concern essences which are instantiated in real individuals. Of real acts of consciousness or of real works of art, or of real moral judgments, we can only come up with contingent truths, truths pertaining for example to their causal and cultural contexts. But we can hope to be able to discover some necessary truths about them only insofar as those truths concern the essences they instantiate. Of the acts of consciousness, for example, we have the allegedly necessary truths about their intentional structure. These truths would hold good, no matter who is the real individual to whom those acts belong or in what sorts of bodily organism, possibly different from ours, they are realized. In this sense, it would be easy to recognize that in some sense or other all philosophy is concerned with essences, with generalities rather than with particular cases. One is accustomed to hearing that philosophical truths are conceptual truths rather than factual ones. The rationale for this claim lies in the expectation that philosophy, or rather phenomenology, must be able to deliver necessary truths (necessary in some sense, to be further explicated). Although the two claims—the claim namely that philosophical truths are conceptual truths and the claim that phenomenological truths are essential truths—are not identical, there is, nevertheless, a close connection between them, a connection which may help us to appreciate the essentialism of phenomenology. This connection is but the connection between "concept" and "essence." It is possible to have a theory of concept—a purely linguistic and conventional theory of concept-formation—which would make the notion of concept totally independent of any commitment to essentialism. But it is possible to have an account according to which a concept is but a subjective mode of presentation of an essence, such that the essence is a *res*, while a concept is in the mind corresponding to the essence. Without pausing to elaborate this thesis, I would presently turn to the question: What, after all, are essences, and how do we know them?

Every individual object is first of all a unique this-there, but in addition it also possesses essential properties which, Husserl tells us, it must have in order that it may have other secondary determinations. A material thing must, for example, have the property of being extended so that it can have any specific shape or size. Likewise, it must have color in general, so that it can be either red or blue or green. Thus, it exemplifies such essences as materiality, extension, rectangularity, color in general, and redness (possibly). Likewise, an intentional act of believing exemplifies the essence "consciousness," it also exemplifies the essence "intentionality," also the essence of being a belief. The particular material thing under consideration, the this-there, is only contingently rectangular or red. Its very existence is also contingent in the sense that although there may be sufficient reasons why it exists rather than not, it is not logically necessary that it exists. Husserl, therefore, says that "Individual Being of every kind is, to speak generally, 'accidental.'"[7] It could be other than what it is. Its physical necessity (in terms of the de facto laws of nature) is quite consistent with its contingency from the logical and essential points of view. However, it is an essential truth that if it is to be material, it must be extended. That the material thing is extended is not contingent. Thus, every individual reality exemplifies essential interconnections. The task of phenomenology is now construed as consisting in discovering such essential truths.

Husserl at this point introduces his concept of ontology. Every real individual comes under a highest "material essence." A material thing, although it instantiates many complicated essential interconnections, comes under the highest essence "material nature." Each such essence defines a region. The science, nonempirical to be sure, of this region is called by Husserl a "regional ontology." Thus, there is a regional ontology of the region "material nature" which would be very different indeed from physics as an empirical science. This regional ontology would rather state the essential truths which obtain amongst the essences which constitute this region. Thus, it would include pure geometry, pure theory of physical time, pure theory of causality, a theory of motion, and a theory of colors, to give a few examples. It would come very close to what Kant calls "pure physics," although it would obviously not be identical with it.

In order to fully understand Husserl's theory of essence, we need to keep before our minds the various kinds of essences that he recognized. Figure 1.1 shows his classification of essences.

Along with the above classifications of essences, it is also necessary to bear in mind Husserl's classification of individuals into real and ideal, and of real individuals into abstract and concrete. Examples of ideal individuals are the number 2 and Beethoven's Fifth Symphony. An example of eidetic singularity is this specific shade of red or also, to take a formal essence, the form *modus ponens*. An eidetic singularity does not have instances, but is itself embodied in a real entity, just as the form "*S* is *P*" is embodied (but not instantiated) in "This chalk is white."

I think Husserl's concept of essence is distinguished from the classical Platonic theories in at least two respects: first, in its recognition of

Figure 1.1

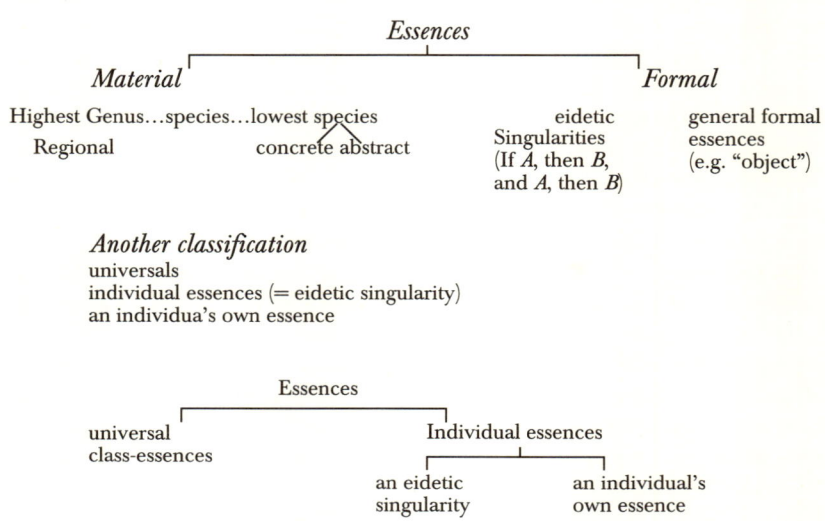

Another classification
universals
individual essences (= eidetic singularity)
an individua's own essence

```
                    Essences
         ┌─────────────┴─────────────┐
     universal              Individual essences
   class-essences         ┌─────────┴─────────┐
                    an eidetic         an individual's
                    singularity         own essence
```

such eidetic singularities; second, in recognizing that an individual has its own essence which is not the essence of another individual. There is a further point of distinction which permits Husserl's theory to be called phenomenological as contradistinguished from the metaphysical theories. I will return to this last point at a later stage of this chapter.

A few comments on the first two distinctions. The eidetic singularities are not to be construed as universals that have instances. They are rather like the Russellian noninstantiated universals which are themselves ingredients of reality at the same time at different spatial locations. Recall Russell's example: "to the north of" is identically the same relation that obtains between Edinburgh and London, as well as between Darjeeling and Calcutta. It is an eidetic singularity. Likewise, picture two regions of space pervaded by the same shade of red. In that case, the same shade of red is both here and there, it is not instantiated.

Now, as to an individual's own essence: consider Socrates. He is an instance of the universal essence "living being," also of "philosopher," as well as of "wisdom." But these universals are also instantiated in other individuals. Is there any essence that is instantiated only in Socrates and in no one else? This is indeed a controversial idea, and the best way to understand the point is to recall the age-old controversy about the principle of individuation. What is it that makes Socrates the unique individual he is? Any form, or universal, it would seem, which is instantiated in Socrates may as well be instantiated in some other individual. It would seem then, that no form could be individuating. Thus, we have the Thomist view that the principle of individuation is matter (in this case, either Socrates's body or his soul). This Thomist view runs through a major line of Western thought including Kant. As opposed to this we have the view of Duns Scotus: namely, that the principle of individuation itself is a form, the form which, in the present case, is capable of being instantiated in Socrates alone. Do we have such a form, and, if so, what is it? One answer is: it is something like what Carnap called the "individual concept." Another answer is that which, it seems, Husserl suggested: consider the entire *what* or *So-sein* of Socrates, including the most specific of the properties he has, then think away his actual existence; what we have then is the total content of the idea of Socrates, his own essence, which according to one of Husserl's well-known definitions, is a *concretum*; it is an essence (a complex one in this case) that can be instantiated by itself without needing any further supplementation. This brings us to Husserl's definition of an individual: it is a this-there whose material (i.e., nonformal) essence is a concretum.[8]

Metaphysicians since ancient times have wondered if it is possible to so specify the forms (from genera to species, from species to their subspecies) that eventually we come down to real individuals. It has appeared to be rather more plausible that however we may specify the forms, we reach the lowest species, the *infima species* which is still in the realm of forms, so that there is no smooth passage from the realm of forms to the realm of real individuals. Husserl seems to have held the view that the entire content, the entire *what* of a real individual, can be regarded as an essence, and that what we thereby abstract from is the mere existence. "Existence" is neither a part of the content or *So-sein* of the thing, nor derives from the matter of the individual as opposed to its form, but rather, in a Kantian vein, is the predicate that derives from an act of positing.

Beyond Essentialism?

At the beginning of this chapter, I traced a trajectory of Husserl's phenomenology that moves from a concern with essences to a concern with meanings, from there to the concept of transcendental subjectivity, finally via the phenomenology of the lifeworld.

In my earlier works I have developed an argument as to how the transition from the essences to meanings is made.[9] In developing this argument, it has not been my intention to impute to Husserl precisely this argument. I have rather tried to reconstruct for myself what has appeared to me to be a pressing reason to abandon essentialism in favor of meanings. The argument runs something like this: if, as many philosophers hold, there are no *de re* essences, if that is to say our determination of the essence of a thing is relative to how we describe that thing (recall Quine's example of a bicyclist who is also a mathematician), then we must abandon the essences as constituting an autonomous realm. What the essence of a thing is would depend upon how we take that thing to be. The latter is precisely the notion of "noema." What is fundamental then is that things are presented in different ways, that we take them differently, or in other words, we regard them as having different meanings (where the concept of "meaning" is transferred from semantics to a larger context). Let us remember that phenomenology wants to be a presuppositionless, descriptive science. Describing essences does not then appear to satisfy that claim. There is the added reason for why it cannot satisfy that claim: our apprehension of the essence of a thing is not free from the possibilities of error and inadequacy. Essences are transcendent entities, transcendent in the sense that they are not components of the immanent realm of our mental life; they rather belong to the world. They therefore suffer from all the inadequacies that characterize transcendent entities as regards their cognitions. Meanings or noemata, however, are inseparable aspects of our mental experiences, so that our hold upon them is sure and certain: I know precisely what I mean, I know for certain what a certain thing presented in my experience meant to me. In other words, as I have an experience, I also know its noema.

Once the shift from essences to meanings is effected, transcendental phenomenology is not far behind. Since it is arguable that meanings are conferred by intentional acts, one understands why Husserl would have held that things, as well as the world, are constituted by consciousness. They all owe the constitution of their senses to the intentional lives of egos.

In the following chapters, I do not propose to follow that line of thinking. Supposing we hold on to the doctrine of *de re* essences. Then we have what may be called a realistic essentialism. Husserl and the early phenomenologists—those of Munich and Göttingen—seem to have upheld such a realism regarding essences. However, the Munich and Göttingen phenomenologists were all disappointed when the master, Husserl himself, turned toward the subjective life of experience. They were convinced that Husserl's turn toward a seemingly Neo-Kantian position meant that he had abandoned the original program of phenomenology as a descriptive science of essences.

In these chapters, I will hold fast to Husserl's essentialism, and then find a way toward his transcendental phenomenology. In order to do that I will consider the views of some of his early students and fellow workers in the field of phenomenology with regard to essences and the consequent realism/idealism issue. I have chosen Scheler and Ingarden, who were close to Husserl's circle, the former an already independent philosopher when he came to be close to the Munich circle, the latter Husserl's pupil. I will then consider Nicolai Hartmann, who was a "critical realist" but whose essentialism was influenced by Husserl's, although he did suggest radical changes in understanding the nature of essences. I could have referred to the views of Pfänder and Reinach in this regard, but I will wait for another occasion to do that.

The Two Reductions

Before I close this chapter, I must recall the distinction, often confused by writers, between eidetic reduction and phenomenological reduction. Eidetic reduction, as the name implies, is that reduction by which one comes to "see and seize upon" (as Fred Kersten puts it) an essence. In brief, the method consists in abstracting from existence, from all *Dasein*, so that what we have before our mental glance, is the existence-free essence in its purity. If every reduction has two aspects to it—namely, something which it puts within brackets and something which it focuses upon as what stands outside the brackets—then in eidetic reduction, what is bracketed is existence and what is left outside the brackets is the essence. An effective component of this method is what is called the method of variation, sometimes called eidetic or imaginative variation. One starts with a typical example—either simply imagined, or a real thing transformed into a merely imaginary one by abstracting from its reality—of the class of entities whose essence one wants to discover. Then one varies, in imagination, its various features until one finds that any further variation is incompatible with the thing's being an instance of the type which it was initially chosen to represent. When we reach the limits of such imaginative variability, we also discover the essence of that type. I have discussed the method along with its limitations and problems in my book *Transcendental Phenomenology: An Analytic Account*.

Phenomenological reduction, on the other hand, abstracts from the transcendent existence of things that are objects of intentional acts, and focuses upon them in the how of their givenness in those acts. To be

brief, in this reduction we put the existence of entities, real or ideal, real individuals or ideal essences, within brackets, and focus upon the noemata in and through which those entities are presented to consciousness. It is this reduction which uncovers that domain of intentional life of subjectivity, with its noetic-noematic structure and its internal temporality. Again, without going into well-known details, one can distinguish between a phenomenological-psychological version of this reduction and a transcendental-phenomenological version, depending upon how radical is one's bracketing of transcendence. One crucial step needs to be noted: while effecting the phenomenological-psychological reduction, one may still construe one's own mental life as possessing psychological reality, belonging to the person who is reflecting, presupposing his bodily and vital natures—in general, one may still leave unquestioned the construal of consciousness as a stratum of the world, founded upon the inorganic and organic strata of nature, and belonging to a real community of other individual persons. Transcendental-phenomenological reduction puts even these so seemingly self-evident beliefs within brackets, and reduces them to beliefs with their truth-claims, within the ego's own mental life. But with the bracketing, and consequent suspension—not denial—of belief in the world, the ego, identically the same ego, becomes a transcendental ego who seeks to uncover within his own reflective and prereflective experiencings the constitution of the sense of the world and of the things in the world.

All the phenomenologists we shall be considering here recognized the worth of the eidetic reduction, although they all construed it differently. None of them went along with the phenomenological reduction, especially in its transcendental dimension. They all rejected the seemingly idealistic implications of Husserl's transcendental phenomenology. Did they correctly understand the motives that led Husserl to his mature transcendental philosophy? At least one, Roman Ingarden, Husserl's faithful pupil, tried hard, all through his life, to understand those motives, and was convinced that somewhere Husserl must have been subject to some conceptual confusion. I will briefly present Ingarden's arguments. In chapter 7, I hope to be able to return to Husserl and consider how he and his critics fare in the long run.

Can an Essentialism be Phenomenological?

Amongst the distinguishing features of Husserl's theory of essences, I had included one, the third in the list, on which I should now make some explanatory comments. In the philosophical tradition deriving from Plato, it is commonplace to correlate the two orders of being—real individuals and Ideas—to two cognitive faculties, sense perception and reason. In making this claim, I leave room for differences of opinion regarding the nature of reason: some regard reason as a faculty of intuition, while others would construe it as a faculty of abstraction. Be that as it may, it is agreed upon in that tradition that real individuals are apprehended in one way, and Ideas or essences in another.

In many respects, Husserl departs from that tradition. I leave out of consideration the question of whether Husserl, in his theory of essences, was a Platonist or an Aristotelian, in other words, whether for him, essences are *ante res* or *in res*. But it must be emphasized that Husserl's epistemological theory does not make use of the two faculty theory that is replaced by him by a very different sort of distinction—namely, that between symbolic meaning intendings and their fulfillment. The former amounts to empty thinking and the latter amounts to authentic, fulfilled and intuitive having the thing before one's glance exactly as it was emptily intended.

What is, however, distinctive about Husserl's theory of essence is that, on his view, it is not philosophers, or phenomenologists, who first come to intuit the essences. On the contrary, we all, in our everyday experiencings of things, also come to see the essences. "The truth is," he writes, "that everyone sees 'ideas,' 'essences' and sees them, so to speak, continuously; they operate with them in their thinking and they also make judgments about them. It is only that, from their theoretical 'standpoint' people interpret them away."[10] Phenomenology only provides a method by which one can come to clearly recognize what one all along has been acquainted with. The reductions teach us to remove those theoretical prejudices that have acquired a kind of unquestioned self-evidence. By removing these prejudices, we are enabled to recognize that we are indeed acquainted, in our everyday experience of the world, not only with real individuals, events, situations, and facts, but also with essences as they are exemplified, instantiated, and embodied in them. Hence, Husserl's remarkably simple but enigmatic statement: "At first, 'essence' indicates that which in the intimate self-being of an individual discloses to us '*what*' it is."[11] This essence, disclosed in empirical intuition, can, however, be transformed, by methodical thinking, into a pure *eidos*: this happens when we no more consider the essence as exemplified in this thing before us, but take it as an object *sui generis* that is independent of the actual and possible instantiations.

We shall have occasions, in these chapters, to raise various philosophical questions regarding this entire theory. But I must end this chapter by stating my belief rather dogmatically: today, under the influence of various philosophical ideas, it is usual to suspect a theory of essence, at least in recent continental thought. At the same time, in recent analytical thinking, the nominalism of the fifties and sixties has been replaced by a fruitful interest in essentialism. So, despite the prevailing antifoundationalisms, theories of flux, historicisms, and deconstructionisms, I must assert that essentialism is alive and well. This is because it is solidly entrenched in our experience and knowledge of the world. We not only experience things as unique particulars, as this-there, but also as being of a certain kind, as exemplifying some fundamental sort, and as subject to very fundamental formal structures. Phenomenologically, essences are undeniable. But what sort of metaphysics they need is quite another question.

More about the Tensions

To return now to the *perceived* tensions in Husserl's thinking: first, the tension between his essentialism and his transcendental philosophy; second, that between his essentialism and transcendental philosophy, on the one hand, and his later historicism, on the other; third, between all these three facets and the thesis about the lifeworld; fourth, between the intuitionism, the resolve to describe the given qua given, and the constitution theory. There is also the conflict between the transcendentalism with its claim to "purify" consciousness of all its empirical "corruptions" and the necessity for the empirical and the corporeal. This last conflict, so forcefully highlighted by Derrida, has many other aspects: one between the purity of the expression and the indispensability of an indicative sign, another between the total presence of the "living present" and the constitutive role of absence within the heart of that living present; still another between the absolutely new beginning of an *Urstiftung* and the continuity of history. Overall, there is the large all-encompassing problem of the relation between the transcendental and the empirical, and the ubiquitous suspicion regarding transcendental phenomenology's overstepping its boundaries into metaphysics.

To "explain" all these problematic aspects of Husserl's thinking would require a careful account of the development of his thinking, on the one hand, and a comprehensive interpretation of his philosophy, on the other. These large tasks cannot be undertaken here. It is also necessary to keep in mind that philosophers who have insisted upon one or other of these internal conflicts come with their own agenda. In these and other regards, Husserl himself is his best critic. Only, he is a more careful critic than most others.

Attempts will be made in these essays to relate the concept of essence to the concept of meaning, and the concept of transcendental subjectivity to the concept of the lifeworld. These two attempts will lead to a proper understanding of the role of history in transcendental phenomenology: in the relevant sense, history has to be a history of constitution of meanings. This will lead to the recognition of discontinuities in history, and even to recognition of the truth in the locution about different times. All these will help us to properly understand the Husserlian distinction between transcendental and empirical subjectivities.

This last distinction is no doubt "enigmatic." In distinguishing between them, and in using the epoché to move from the one to the other, Husserl asserts a difference. He also affirms their identity: the empirical *is* the transcendental, only when stripped of the naturalizing interpretations. More famously, he affirms a parallelism between the two: each numerically selfsame intentional experience of an empirical ego is also a transcendental experience of the "corresponding" transcendental ego. To think these aspects of the relation—identity, difference, and parallelism—together would appear to be baffling. And yet, we do not understand transcendental phenomenology if we do not understand this enigma. To this I will turn in the concluding note to chapter 9.

2

Max Scheler's Theory of Knowledge

Max Scheler, more known for his moral theory, also developed a highly interesting theory of knowledge which, primarily based upon certain insights of Husserl, incorporated important elements from other sources, and so appears to make up for the onesidedness of the Husserlian conception of knowledge. Dilthey had remarked that in the veins of the knowing subject as constructed by Locke, Hume, and Kant, there was no real blood, but only an impoverished juice of reason as mere thinking. What he wanted was to take into account the entire man with all his powers, thinking, willing, and feeling. Scheler may be said to be the one philosopher whose theory of knowledge takes this Diltheyan need into account. Knowledge involves not merely theoretical reason, but also moral and other practical interests. Scheler's task is one of how to take all this into account without falling into superficial pragmatism.

Let us begin with what may be regarded as his fundamental premise. Everything that is, has two aspects, its *Dasein* and its *Sosein*, its *that* and its *what*, its existence and, if you like, its content. These two aspects are distinguishable, but are they separable? Scheler insists that both idealism and what is called in modern German thought "critical realism" (defended, for example, by Nicolai Hartmann) have this much in common: that both regard these two aspects in a thing to be inseparable. Since the two are taken to be inseparable, idealism regards the entire thing, with its that and its what, to be in the mind, while critical realism holds that both are outside the mind, while in the mind that knows the thing there is a picture or an image of the thing. Scheler rejects both views. Idealism is wrong in thinking that the thing, together with its that and its what, is in the mind, while it is right in holding that when a thing is known, its *Sosein* is replicated in the mind while still remaining outside. Critical realism is right in insisting that the thing, together with its that and its what, is outside the mind. It is wrong in thinking that since the two aspects of the thing are inseparable, and since the that of the thing must be outside the mind, so also must the what, as a consequence of which what the mind possesses, when knowing a thing, is an image of the thing. As a matter of fact, the image, even if it is present, is useless. It is not intentional, it cannot relate the mind to its object, and it cannot confer on the mind its intentional reference to its object.

Scheler's thesis then is that the two aspects of a thing are indeed separable. The function of spirit (*Geist*) precisely consists in separating the two, in freeing the *Sosein* from its *Dasein*—a position not unlike F. H. Bradley's well-known view that thought consists in letting the content loose from its existence (and then predicating this ideal content of reality),[1] only this latter half of Bradley's view (which makes the task of thought so futile) is absent in Scheler. In all knowledge, the *Sosein* is both outside the mind (in the thing) and in the mind. It is not a picture of the *Sosein* that is in the mind, it is the *Sosein* itself that is also outside in the thing. It is this remarkable achievement of the mind that Scheler regards as the essence of knowing. In this sense, knowing is an ontological relation: one entity, the knowing mind, partakes (*teilhaben*) in the other, the thing. This participation, at first prereflective, is *Wissen*; subsequently, it is reflective knowing, i.e., *Erkennen*. In the most general sense, then, knowing is taking part in being, taking *part* literally (thus presupposing, as Scheler tells us, the ontological relation of whole and part),[2] the known becoming a part of the knower. This relation is neither spatial nor temporal nor causal. (It is not clear then how the relation can be one of part and whole. Obviously, we need a conception of part and whole, which is not spatial.) What happens, according to Scheler, is that a *Sosein* that is not intentional becomes one that is intentional. In spite of this change, there is strict identity. The prereflective knowing is also called by Scheler "ecstatic." Consciousness presupposes this ecstatic participation in reality. Consciousness therefore is not originary; it is founded upon an ontological relation. Thus far, Scheler's view anticipates Heidegger's.

In another respect, Scheler's theory of knowledge appropriates an important element from Husserl. Reportedly, Scheler first met Husserl in Halle in 1901. Husserl referred him to his view of "intuition" in the *Logische Untersuchungen*. Scheler immediately recognized there something he was already looking for, a conception of intuition that is not restricted to sensory perception. As is well known, Husserl had extended "intuition" to include not only sensory perception, but also intuition of essences and what he calls "categorial intuition" (i.e., intuition of logically formed states of affairs).³ For Scheler, this conception is of decisive importance. What is common to all modes of intuition, according to Husserl, is that in intuition the object of knowledge is itself *bodily* given. Taking this conception in the strict sense, Scheler excludes all sensory perception from the scope of genuine intuition, as also all scientific knowledge—for reasons we shall soon state. In the strict sense, phenomenological knowledge of essences alone is intuitive. We shall return to this very controversial position.

One more general remark, before we enter into the details of this theory. Scheler is one of the few philosophers in the Western tradition who clearly and explicitly developed an account of the *moral* conditions of knowing.⁴ Since knowledge, especially philosophical knowledge, as we shall see, requires giving oneself over to things as they are, one needs to cultivate an attitude whereby one frees oneself from the natural impulses and desires, including the impulse to dominate and use beings, including nature, to one's own advantage. This is what Scheler likes to call "love."⁵ Besides love, one needs also to cultivate humility, whereby one becomes open and sensitive to the essential nature of beings. One also needs self-control in the sense that one does not let one's subjective preferences interfere in the letting-be of the objective content of reality, whatever that may be. Thus, love, humility, and self-control are the three moral virtues one needs to cultivate in order to be able to know in the strictly phenomenological sense.

Today, when knowledge has become technical, this entire idea that in order to be able to do philosophy one needs to develop certain moral attitudes will be rejected perhaps by most philosophers. But I do not want to set it aside as entirely beside the point, convinced as I am that the spirit of competitiveness and aggressiveness which vitiates intellectual life of today has ruinous consequences for philosophy as a whole.

This brings me to Scheler's interpretation of Husserl's famed method of reduction.

Types of Knowledge

Scheler divides knowledge into several kinds. These divisions are not always made by him in the same way. The more common division is into: *Bildungswissen* (knowledge which is meant for the development of the person who knows); *Erlösungswissen* (knowledge whose purpose is salvation); and *Herrschafts-* or *Leistungswissen* (knowledge whose goal is practical domination and transformation of the world for our human ends). The object of the second kind of knowledge is God, the ground of all beings. The first, *Bildungswissen*, includes the cultural sciences, but in the long run consists in philosophy as knowledge of the essences. The last, i.e., knowledge of control and achievement, includes natural scientific knowledge and technology.

At other places, especially in his essay "The Theory of Three Facts,"[6] Scheler distinguishes between the natural worldview, philosophical knowledge, and the natural sciences, and goes on to work out a way of distinguishing between their respective objects as well as the natures of the three kinds of cognition.

For my present purpose, I will confine my exposition of Scheler's theory of knowledge to three kinds of knowledge in a manner which cuts across these other divisions, but which is directly relevant to my purpose. These three are: sense perception, natural science, and philosophy. To each of these Scheler devotes an enormous amount of careful work, and his views about perception and science are of great interest and contemporary relevance. He also, rightly in my view, insists that a theory of knowledge must include a theory of philosophical knowledge, something which most epistemologists either overlook or reject and an issue in which Scheler seems to have been influenced by Emil Lask.[7]

Sense Perception

Accounts of sense perception usually start with a theory of what precisely is given in sense perception, although they may differ in their answers to this question. As is well known, some philosophers regard the sensory data as what are given, while others regard the physical object itself to be given. Scheler begins by preferring the latter: the complete material thing with a definite spatial form is given. The so-called sensations are only names for "variable relations between bodily conditions and the phenomena of the external or internal world."[8] Sensations are relative to the organization of the body. How then do sensations stand in relation to the facts of the natural world? Scheler's thesis here is rather complicated. The following may serve as a brief account: the commonly accepted idea that sensations are effects of the external world on us is completely mistaken, inasmuch as it confuses physics with physiology. The given facts of external perception can be equally well explained by physics as by physiology or biology. The given state of affairs is simultaneously a sign for a physical and a physiological process. The data of cognition are not furnished by the sensory functions. They are rather furnished by a unitary act of intuition performed by means of these functions. The sensory functions only select those aspects of external reality that can serve as signs for the vital functions that preserve the body. The body does not determine, e.g., the contents of "red" or "blue." The body rather determines the fact that such a content becomes a sign for the thing. The sensory functions make known to the organism the presence or absence of external things surrounding the organism. The sense organs serve their specific functions against the general background of the sensitivity of the entire body. When the dialogue between the body and the world takes place and the sensory functions play their roles of selection of data in the interests of the organism's survival, they trigger off, as it were, the cognitive act of pure intuition of the thing out there.

Clearly, in this account Scheler is trying to accommodate several considerations. Husserl had already argued convincingly that we do not, in perception, infer the existence of the external object behind the sensory data. To the contrary, we perceive the physical object itself, only from a certain perspective. Thus, a phenomenological description of perception was showing that the idea of "sensation" is a theoretical construct—as Merleau-Ponty later argued.[9] For another, there is the role that external perception plays in the survival of the organism—here Scheler draws upon evolutionary biology and a general pragmatic orientation. In between the two—the completed act of perceiving an external thing and the biological function of fulfilling the needs of the body—stand the sensory functions whose role is not presenting, but only analytical—either to select or to suppress data which serve as signs, on the one hand, for the thing out there and, on the other, for a state of the organism.

What, in effect, Scheler is aiming at is to reconcile a phenomenological description of perceptual experience with evolutionary biology and a gestalt theoretic account of perception. Sensation is not a phenomenon,[10] nor a constituent of our perceptual content, but rather a condition for the coming into being of perception. The so-called "constancy theory" (namely, that there is a proportionality between stimulus and sensation) and the assumption of "unnoticed sensations" have to be given up. Even the simplest perception is accompanied by motor impulses. An organism's picture of the world has as its alphabets only those sensory qualities which can serve as signs for objects, which are important for that organism's instinctive and motor relations.[11]

I must emphasize that this is only a brief summary, in bare outlines, of the salient aspects of Scheler's theory of perception. A detailed study of it would not only show an interesting attempt to combine phenomenology with science, but would demonstrate the way Scheler anticipated the work to be done after him by such investigators as Aron Gurwitsch, Merleau-Ponty, and Erwin Strauss.

Scientific Knowledge

Like Husserl in the *Crisis*, Scheler also contrasts the scientific world with what he calls the world of the natural outlook. Whereas the latter is the world of perceived things and qualities, the scientific world consists, according to him, of "states of affairs." Things and events, in the scientific world, are bearers of "states of affairs"—they are not perceived but constructed. The scientific fact is something new, emerging out of the dissolution of the things of the everyday world. Scientific observation replaces ordinary perception, and technical experiment replaces natural experimentation.

Both the objects of ordinary perception and of the scientific world are transcendent in the sense that they do not coincide with the phenomenological contents of the corresponding acts (of perception and observation, respectively). They are both indirectly given, where "indirect" or mediated givenness should not be misconstrued as "inferred." The natural spherical thing—the round ball I perceive—needs to be "scientifically reduced" (Scheler now speaks of a "scientific reduction" as distinguished from "phenomenological reduction").[12] The "appearance" of the natural object (i.e., the side turned toward me) is now regarded—in the "scientific reduction"—as a symbol of the entire round object, as also of a "state" within me. The objectively existing sphere is itself not intuited, but posited, so also the "state" of the organism. They are not *given* to each other, but causally interact within objective nature. The objectively existing sphere is posited through a mathematical construction, in accordance with a definition, of a geometrical sphere, or of a metal.

To this account of scientific fact, Scheler adds a further component: scientific facts, for their facthood, presuppose the institution of science as an evolving social condition. This institution includes, amongst others, the requirement that the putative scientific facts must be capable of being *produced* by technology, and the concepts and propositions expressing them must be communicable and verifiable, not universally, but by the members of the scientific community.

Finally, scientific knowledge, on Scheler's view, is motivated not by the ideal of pure theory (as Husserl took it to be), but by the goal of practical control and domination. It is, in this context, that we may also recall Scheler's extensive discussion of pragmatism (of Peirce, James, and Dewey, as well as of Schiller) in his essay "Erkenntnis und Arbeit."[13] He recognizes the truths in pragmatism: that the primary relation of man to world is not theoretical, but practical; that natural perception is determined by practical interests; that the epistemic goal of the positive natural sciences is controlled manipulation and domination of nature. As regards science, a natural phenomenon, Scheler writes, is regarded as "known" if the science can come up with a plan in accordance with which that phenomenon, in its determinate *hic et nunc*, can be reproduced or can be thought of as produced (through a real or a thought-experiment).[14] He can therefore say: "Nicht der 'reine Verstand,' nicht der 'reine Geist' entwarf zu beginn der Neuzeit . . . das gewaltige programm einer allseitigen mechanischen Natur—und Seelenerklärung, sondern der auf die *Natur* zielende neue *Macht*—und *Arbeitswille einer neu aufsteigende Gesellschaft.*"[15] In spite of recognizing the value of pragmatism, Scheler severely takes it to task for its "banal utilism," but also for its inability to give an account of pure philosophical knowledge.

Philosophical Knowledge

Scheler's account of philosophical knowledge is determined by his conception of phenomenology as a descriptive science of essences. In the preceding essay, we looked briefly at the theory of essence underlying all that, and even that brief consideration must have brought out the fact that there are many unclarified and subtle aspects of that theory. Although Scheler makes the phenomenological theory of essence the central focus of his own conception of philosophy, he is surprisingly unhelpful if we attempt to develop the theory of essence. The few things he tells us about essences are perhaps these:

An essence is not a concept that is abstracted from individual instances,[16] and intuition of essences is not an inductive generalization. A genuine essence, he claims, cannot be defined without circularity: examples are "Spirit" (*Geist*) and "Life."[17] An essence is a pure whatness; it is in itself neither universal nor individual.[18] An essential connection (that, e.g., a promise ought to be kept) cannot be proved,[19] but has to be intuited. Scheler does not help us very much if we ask what this whatness is. Here we have to turn to Ingarden.

But Scheler's theory of essences, and of philosophical knowledge of them, has several peculiar features which mark his position off from Husserl's.

In the first place, whereas Husserl thought that intuition of an essence presupposes, and is founded upon, sensuous intuition of an individual that exemplifies or embodies that essence (or, upon an imaginary instance visualized in imagination),[20] Scheler insisted that the intuition of essences is presupposed by the sensory perception of individuals. Essences, as he puts it, are pregiven, and he takes Husserl to task for making sense perception (or its modification, imagination) the foundation of eidetic intuition.[21] I believe that what Scheler means by his claim that essences are pregiven is that in order to be able to perceive the thing over there as a living being, or a person over there as a person, one must already be intuiting, or have intuition of, the senses "living being" and "spirit." This is actually not very different from—although it is not identical with—a claim Husserl makes (which I recalled in chapter 1)—namely, that everyone, not phenomenologists alone, intuits essences, although this intuition is covered up by prejudices and interpretations. What is important, however, is to determine in what sense of "essence" this claim is defensible.

Furthermore, Scheler regards our intuition of essences as nonsymbolic and nonlinguistic, as contrasted with sense perception and scientific knowledge. Husserl, on the contrary, insisted on a "thoroughgoing analogy" between sensuous intuition and eidetic intuition: in both, something is itself "bodily given," in the former a real individual thing, in the latter an essence or an essential interconnection. For Husserl, any intuition is a nonsymbolic experience in which the thing itself is given, but also any *knowledge* is an experience in which an intuition "fills" a prior empty, merely symbolic, intention. So, insofar as an essential intuition can claim to be a knowledge, it will involve language, and can be appropriately articulated.

A further difference concerns Scheler's interpretation of the phenomenological (in this case, the *eidetic*) reduction, which—he agreed with Husserl—is necessary for philosophy, but which, he thought, Husserl did not quite adequately describe and theorize about. (This, I must add, is partly true, for Husserl did not so much focus on eidetic reduction, although he was constantly using it, as on the later developed transcendental reduction.) Husserl's insufficient grasp of the nature of eidetic reduction, according to Scheler, is due to his unclear, and even false, theory of reality. In the reduction, one is supposed to abstract from the aspect of reality or existence, and let the essence stand out as the focus of reflective grasp. So far so good, but, on Scheler's view, Husserl had a rather simplistic theory of reality: whatever is temporal, i.e., in time, is, for him, real. Husserl also used another characterization: the real individual is originally grasped in sense perception. Both of these are, as formulated, rejected by Scheler.[22]

What Husserl's thinking lacks, and what Scheler claims to give, is a theory of the technique that is needed to bracket, suspend, and put out of action the experience of reality. Husserl saw it, rather too simplistically, as a logical act, to be performed in an instantaneous act of decision. What is decisive is rather the question (which Husserl never asked) of how reality, existence, *Dasein* is experienced, how it is given: the much-discussed question of *Realitätsgegebenheit*. Scheler, in this regard, belongs to a long line of thinkers—whose ancestry goes back to Fichte and Schopenhauer, and the British psychologists—for whom our sense of real existence derives from the experience of resistance to volition (not, as Husserl thought, from sense perception): this experience of reality is preconscious. To be real is to be capable of being efficacious (*wirkungsfähig*). The will, which meets resistance from reality, is rooted in the biological drives (*Lebensdrang*). If we were simply intellectual beings, idealism could not be refuted. Realism is grounded in our vital and volitional nature. Scheler called himself a "voluntaristic realist." (Recall Santayana's thesis that the reality of the external world is grounded not on reason, but on "animal faith.")

Given this account of *Realitätsgegebenheit* (a topic on which both Heidegger and Hartmann wrote, but originally, of course, Dilthey), the reduction of the positing of reality can consist only of a spiritual technique by which one inhibits, puts out of operation, the vital drives in which will is grounded. The name that Scheler almost always recalls in this context is Gautama, the Buddha. The *Lebensdrang* can be inhibited only by a desireless *love*, a loving giving oneself over to the timeless essences of things, a spiritual act of asceticism in which spirit (*Geist*) conquers life. Phenomenology as a knowledge of essences is a victory of spirit. *Geist*, in all cognition, separates the what from the that, but only in phenomenology is this achieved through a technique.

Husserl saw to it that neither his theory of essences nor his account of transcendental subjectivity be construed as a metaphysical thesis. Scheler wanted his eventual metaphysics to be founded on his theory of essences. Knowledge of essences constitutes, for "philosophical metaphysics," Scheler writes (quoting an expression from Hegel), the "window to the Absolute" (*"Fenster ins Absolute"*).[23]

As against Husserl, the transcendence of all objects of knowledge is maintained: of real things (encountered in the experience of resistance), of essences (intuited in essential intuition), of values (experienced in emotional-valuational acts), and of God (intuited in religious experience). The distinction, and yet correlation, of act and object is scrupulously preserved. Scheler became the leader of the critics of Husserl's seemingly Neo-Kantian *"Bewusstseins-idealismus."*

General Remarks

No account of Scheler's theory of knowledge can be complete without discussion of his theories about knowledge of values and about knowledge of other minds. However, I had to restrict this chapter to those aspects of his theory of knowledge that are directly relevant to the larger idea of a transcendental theory of essences, as sketched in chapter 1.

I think that Scheler's account of the relation between cognition and action—an account which scrupulously steers clear of the extremes of purely intellectual accounts of knowledge and the "banal utilism" of some pragmatists, his theory of our experience of reality in resistance to will (i.e., of the fundamental role of will in experience of reality), and of the general idea that in some way moral virtues may be relevant to philosophical thinking—all these are, in my view, theses of great value. In his works he has also shown, in an exemplary manner, how phenomenology and sciences (in his case, biology, anthropology, and sociology) can be blended in one's thinking. In this regard, his example has been followed by Gehlen, Plessner, and Merleau-Ponty. His distinction between the various ends/goals of cognition has been revived by Habermas in his distinction between different cognitive interests.[24]

However, highly questionable is his understanding of the eidetic reduction as requiring a complete break with the experience of reality. Such a break, even if that is possible within the scope of philosophizing (without introducing into philosophy ascetic techniques in which, I gather from Plessner, Scheler was deeply interested), leaves us with a domain of essences cut off from the world, and so without the ability to provide any explanation of the world's being what it is. It must be remembered that Husserl did not want reduction to be a breaking loose, a *real* separation, from reality. He only required an abstraction from the aspect of real existence. He saw clearly that even after the bracketing of existence-positing, what is left is the *Sosein* of an individual, an individual's what, which we seize upon. It then requires a further "change of attitude" ("*Blickwendung*") to be able to focus upon a nonindividual, general entity—the mental process needed is called "ideational or generalizing abstraction" or simply "ideation." Thus, in the *Logische Untersuchungen*, Husserl wrote: "So erfassen wir die spezifische Einheit Röte direkt, 'selbst,' auf Grund einer singulären Anschauung von etwas Rotem. Wir blicken auf das Rotmoment hin, vollziehen aber einen eigenartigen Akt, dessen Intention auf die 'Idee,' auf das 'Allgemeine,' gerichtet ist."[25] Here we have, in brief, an account of the movement of consciousness from a red thing to the red as a component of its *Sosein*, i.e., as its real property, then to the total (empirical) essence of that thing (after abstraction), and finally to redness as a universal idea independent of any instantiation or embodiment.

Husserl's essentialism was in many ways closer to an enriched empiricism, and that is borne out not only by the considerations just advanced, but also by another difference between his view and Scheler's on these matters. Scheler so radically removed eidetic research from experience that on his view intuition of essences is absolutely indubitable, such that no experience could ever contradict it. On Scheler's view, if I have intuition of the essence of "art," for example, or of "religion," no further, new empirical datum could count against it, for if it did, then this datum could not be a case of art or of religion. The claim to have seized upon the essence is made secure as against any new datum. Husserl kept his mind open: if a putative claim to have identified an essence is contradicted by a new example or a new imaginative variation, then that claim has to be taken back.[26] Thus Husserl, in spite of himself, left room for an open-endedness in eidetic research.

3

Nicolai Hartmann's Phenomenological Ontology

Nicolai Hartmann came from the Marburg School of Neo-Kantians. A student of Hermann Cohen and Paul Natorp, Hartmann came under the influence of Husserl's phenomenology, Meinong's *Gegenstandstheorie*, and other assorted tendencies which, contrary to the Neo-Kantians, emphasized ontology (one such influential work being Hans Pichler's *Über Christian Wolffs Ontologie*).

Ontology should begin, according to Hartmann, "[*in einer*] *gewissen diesseits-Stellung zu den metaphysischen Problemgehalten.*" That is to say, it should begin at a point which is prior to metaphysical problems and positions. It should also be indifferent to the oppositions between philosophical standpoints and systems. The question of "being" is "neutral" as to questions such as: Is there a ground of the world? Does the world's structure exhibit intelligence? The question of "being" has to be faithful to the phenomena; it shall not make hypotheses. It has to be "indifferent" to the realism-idealism controversy. For Hartmann, this indifference implies that while "being" is not reducible to "being an object for a subject," ontology cannot rule out the possibility that there is a being, a subject, for whom the world is an object.

Hartmann recognizes that phenomenology wanted to free philosophy from all such historical oppositions, and to return to the "facts themselves." But, on his view, phenomenology remained preoccupied with "modes of givenness," could not extricate itself from them, and therefore was not able to focus on the entities themselves. To be concerned with modes of givenness is to be adopting the reflective stance of *intentio obliqua*. Hartmann wants ontology to take up the *intentio recta*, which is the natural cognitive attitude.[1]

That being is not being-an-object, whether of consciousness or of knowledge, is borne out, according to Hartmann, by the fact that in every knowledge there is an awareness that the object of that knowledge is more than what is being known in it, that is to say, that there is an "unknown" in it, a limit to intelligibility. These limits to knowledge are not to be construed as limits to being. Being of entities, thus, is *not exhausted* by any feature which derives from a possible relatedness to a subject. With this thesis, Hartmann rejects Husserlian restriction of the question of being to the question of being-given-to-a-pure-ego, but he claims to be retaining the true spirit of phenomenology by preserving the *intentio recta* of the original natural standpoint. The Heideggerian transformation of the ontological problem of being to the *meaning* of being is also rejected on the same ground: it makes the meaning of being relative to an entity (in Heidegger's case, to *Dasein*; in Husserl's case, to a transcendental ego).[2]

Fundamental Distinctions

Positioning himself in this natural *intentio recta*, Hartmann regards ontology to be concerned with: (1) the two aspects ("moments") of being: *Dasein* and *Sosein*, or *that* and *what*; (2) the two spheres of being: *real* and *ideal*; and (3) the modalities of being: *actuality, possibility*, and *necessity*.

One of the errors of phenomenology—including both Husserl's and Scheler's—is that when it regards itself as investigation into essences, as distinguished from existence (as a consequence of eidetic reduction), it forgets that essences also have their *Dasein* (existence) and their *Sosein*, that *Dasein* is not as such real existence. There is also, as with essences and mathematical idealities such as numbers, and values, ideal *Dasein*. Husserl does sometimes insist that essences are a kind of objects *sui generis*, so it may be just right to interpret eidetic reduction not as abstracting from existence, but as abstracting from *real* existence. But, then there is the curious consequence that essences have both real and ideal existence (when they are taken in their purity). Hartmann seems to have wavered on this question. In his early work *Grundzüge einer Metaphysik der Erkenntnis*, he denied existence and individuality to ideal entities, but still ascribed to them *Ansichsein*, intrinsic being.[3] In *Die Grundlegung der Ontologie*, he ascribed existence to them, but that only means he was taking "existence" and "*Ansichsein*" as being the same.

So, for Hartmann, the *Dasein-Sosein* distinction is not quite the same as real-ideal distinction. In addition, Hartmann insisted that some *Sosein*s are "neutral" as against both real and ideal existence: "roundness" belongs to a real spherical ball as well as a geometrical circle.

If concerns (1) and (2) do not coincide, it is also a mistake to collapse (2) with (3). The latter mistake is committed by those who hold that reality is the domain of all that is actual, while essences are pure possibilities. A corollary of this view is that truths about reality (i.e., about what is actual) are contingent, whereas truths about essences (i.e., about pure possibilities) are necessary. This is a widely held view, and one of Hartmann's important theses is that this view is based on an inadequate analysis of *modal* concepts.

Hence the importance of modal concepts in Hartmann's thinking. It is only the modal concepts as pertaining to a sphere of being, which explicate the precise mode of being of that sphere. In other words, Hartmann held that while in an important sense we cannot say much about what "real existence" (or "ideal existence") consists in, the best we can do in this regard is to look at how the concepts of "possibility" "actuality," and "necessity" (and their opposites) behave with regard to the domain of reality (or, with regard to the domain of ideality). So we shall turn to his modal theory, but before I do that, perhaps a quick sketch of what he counts as belonging to the two domains would be in order.

The real world is a stratified structure, on Hartmann's view, with nonliving matter at the base, living organisms founded on it, mental reality founded on organic life, and spirit or *Geist* (including society and all social formations) at the apex. Each of these strata has its own categorial structure, and the entire domain of reality also has certain common structures.

The domain of idealities consists of: mathematical entities (such as numbers), essences, and values. None of the idealities is spatiotemporally individuated. An ideality may be instantiated or be an ingredient in many real individuals, without surrendering its own identity.

Besides these two primary spheres of being, Hartmann also recognized two intermediate (or hybrid) spheres: those of logic and cognition. With this brief sketch, let us look at his modal theory worked out in *Möglichkeit und Wirklichkeit*.[4]

Modal Theory

Hartmann's point of departure for his modal theory is the idea that modal concepts (as well as the relationships between the various modalities) vary from one domain of being to another. Much of classical metaphysics, he points out, errs by not distinguishing the modalities of one sphere from those of another. To take one important example: Leibniz held that more is possible than is actual, that truths of fact are contingent while the truths of reason are necessary. Hartmann insists—recalling a view of stoic and megaric logic—that this Leibnizian thesis seeks to apply to *reality* concepts of possibility and necessity that belong to the domain of ideal essences, logic, and mathematics. It is only then that one regards reality to be actuality and as lacking in necessity. But the necessity it lacks is a necessity that has its home in the domain of idealities. As a matter of fact, the domain of reality has its own sort of necessity, its own modes of possibility and actuality. The same is true of the other sphere as well.

We should therefore distinguish real-possibility, real-actuality, and real-necessity from ideal-possibility, ideal-actuality, and ideal-necessity. Let us consider *possibility*. In the ideal world (i.e., the realm of idealities), the possibility of A is compatible with the possibility of non-A. In the real world, the possibility of A excludes the possibility of non-A. The domain of essences is structured as genus and species. Under one genus, there are many coordinate, but incompatible species. Looked at from the point of view of the genus, all the species are equally possible. In the domain of reality, however, for an event A to be possible means that the entire chain of conditions that bring A about is completed; only then A becomes possible (and non-A impossible). But A also thereby becomes actual. Thus, in the sphere of reality, the possibility of A and the actuality of A coincide. What is not actual, non-A, is really impossible (although the concept of it may still be ideally possible). It also follows, from the above thesis, that a real event A, when it becomes possible and actual (because the totality of conditions bringing it about is given), also becomes necessary—not, to be sure, logically necessary, but really necessary. Thus, in the sphere of reality, possibility, actuality, and necessity coincide. Contrary to traditional metaphysics, Hartmann questions if the domain of essences is one of thoroughgoing necessity. To the contrary, in the genus-species structure, necessity obtains vertically upwards from species to genus (e.g., if one is a human, he/she must be an animal), not from genus to species, nor amongst coordinate species under the same genus. The modality of necessity is limited in the ideal sphere in still more interesting ways: for example, it is restricted to a compossible system, but does not obtain amongst various compossible systems. Contingency appears at the beginning of a system, with the choice of axioms, as for example in the case of a logical system.

For my present purpose, I will restrict myself only to this much of Hartmann's thesis. It runs directly counter to Husserls' well-known thesis in the *Ideas* I: namely, that (1) the domain of essences is one of necessity, and (2) the domain of facts is one of contingency. If Hartmann's thesis is correct, then every real event is necessary, i.e., possesses real-necessity (even if the concept of it may be ideally contingent), and the domain of essences is not characterized by thoroughgoing necessity. It would also be misleading to hold that the domain of essences is one of pure possibilities, whereas the domain of reality is one of mere actuality. For just as the really actual *A* is also really possible, so the ideally possible essence has also its own ideal actuality. (It may be necessary to impose limitations on this last claim with regard to mathematical existence, for if you are an intuitionist, you may not want to ascribe to a mathematical entity existence only if it is consistent; you would want to be able to construct it or find a rule of construction.)

Given this modal theory, the real world cannot any longer be conceived, à la Leibniz, as a selection from many ideal possibilities. The relation between the two spheres has to be construed differently. There is no doubt that the two are interwoven, and that between the categories of the one and those of the other, there is partial identity—which ontology has to precisely describe.

Is Hartmann's thesis of real-necessity acceptable? As I was sitting near my window and writing, it began to rain. On Hartmann's thesis, "It's beginning to rain on the University of Puerto Rico campus at 9:00 A.M. on 11 February 1991" is an event which, at 8:59 A.M. on that day at that place was really impossible, but the next minute became at once possible, actual, and necessary, so that "It's not raining" at that place, at that moment becomes both impossible and nonactual. So a real entity or event, of which Hartmann's modal categories real-possibility, etc. hold good, is a happening here and now. An example of it is not "rainfall," but "raining here and now," not a stone or a mountain, but "This stone's over there beginning to role down the hill now." For only of such an event can you say that all its causal antecedents having taken place the event is necessitated. But if you specify the event down to its spatial and temporal particularity can you any longer speak of its causal conditions? To say that *A* is the cause, or a causal condition, of *B*, is to say that if *A*, then *B*; this locution implies the repeatability of both *A* and *B*. But if *A* and *B* are real events of Hartmann's conception, they cannot by their very nature be meaningfully thought as repeatable. Can we then speak of the causal conditions of a *real* event in this sense?

There is something still very peculiar about this conception of a *real* entity. The idea of its really existing here and now is included in the very idea of such an entity. Note that this is not the classical notion of *ens*, which is defined by Christian Wolff thus: "*ens est quod existere potest*" ("being is that which is capable of existing"). Hartmann would rather *define* it as that which exists. It is not self-evidently obvious that existence should belong to the concept of an entity, since the expression "an entity" would then, purely as an expression, mean something of which it holds good that it exists. This is a strange consequence. On the classical theory, a finite entity such as "a man" exists, *if it exists*. It is something which is capable of existing, and therefore also one which is also capable of not existing.

As a matter of fact, if one continues to try to understand Hartmann's position that "This stone over there is beginning to roll down under the impact of that strong wind," any putative condition of this unique event's existence would be part of the content of this event's uniqueness. The total chain of conditions of the event *B* would in fact be the chain of determinations of its content, i.e., of its real essence. As a consequence, every such real event has to be *causa sui*.

I will not pursue this most interesting thesis to its extreme absurd consequences.[5] I want only to insist that Hartmann's thesis, despite its novelty, leads him to a sort of ontological argument for the existence of every real entity, by making existence a part of its very concept. So I find the classical notion, defended by Husserl, less trouble-free and more intelligible.[6]

A Critique of the Separation of Spheres

An absolute separation of the spheres of being, the real and the ideal, in the manner Hartmann does it, raises serious questions about knowledge of reality as such. It is not for nothing that the this-there, the unique event, has traditionally never been the subject matter of theory, even of scientific theory. Scientific and philosophical theories have been concerned with entities *such as this*. Recall that Aristotle's syllogism does not include a singular proposition as a premise. A singular proposition does not belong to "apophantic logos." The real, stripped of all ideal elements and essences, is nothing but a mere *this*. How then is reality as such known? Not unlike Scheler, Hartmann holds that the primary mode of givenness of reality is emotional and volitional. To understand his position as well as his defense of realism, it is necessary to bear in mind that for him knowing is a transcendent act, i.e., an act that escapes from the confines of consciousness and establishes contact with a reality (or ideality) that exists in itself. Husserlian intentionality holds good of all acts, and not only of knowing. Since acts of knowing are also intentional, they, like all acts of consciousness, have their own intentional objects. But knowledge goes beyond the intentional object—the noema—and grasps (*erfasst*) the transcendent being. This is the truth of realism. A cognitive phenomenon itself—and not a theory about it—points toward an independently existing real being.

There are two other cognitive phenomena, according to Hartmann, which also support realism. These are what he calls "problem-consciousness" and "progress of knowledge." By "problem" he means the as-yet-unknown in the very texture of the object. What is known points beyond itself to what is yet unknown. The content of knowledge brings with it a consciousness of its own inadequacy: the Socratic knowledge of one's ignorance. The other phenomenon characterizes the gradual overcoming of this inadequacy, namely, an awareness of the progress of knowledge.

However, knowing is not the only transcendent act. Knowledge is rooted, according to Hartmann, in emotional-receptive acts as well as in emotional-prospective acts: both being inseparable from the interconnected contexture of life, the *Lebenszusammenhang*, which binds men to their world. The emotional-receptive acts are the acts of *Erleben* (experiencing), *Erleiden* (suffering), and *Ertragen* (endurance), in all of which something presses itself against the subject so that the subject experiences resistance. They all bring to the forefront what Hartmann calls the stubbornness of reality, *die Härte des Realen*. Against Scheler, Hartmann insists that the experience of resistance is not the only way we encounter reality. There are other emotional acts that are not to be brought under that general type. The emotional-prospective acts anticipate the future course of events: acts of hope and readiness (for what is coming) are examples.

But these are only bare outermost experiences, which are generally embedded in larger and larger contexts—eventually in the overall context of the entire universe and human destiny. Our present purpose, however, is to point out how Hartmann uses these phenomena as evidence for a large realistic metaphysics. What Hartmann does not recognize is that however these emotional and volitional acts may point to a transcendent reality, any cognition of that reality must be articulated in conceptual terms, thereby importing idealities into its structure. The problem is a consequence of the separation of the spheres. What we need is some satisfactory way of locating the essences within the content of the "what," of the real this-there.

4

Roman Ingarden's Critique of Husserl's Transcendental Phenomenology

Roman Ingarden was Husserl's pupil, and remained in lifelong contact with him, continuously questioning Husserl's positions, especially his transcendental idealism. Whereas the members of the Munich and Göttingen schools simply abandoned the master as having deviated from the path of philosophy as a rigorous science, Ingarden continued his efforts to understand the motives and the arguments which led Husserl in that direction. In this relentless effort, he seems to have gone a long way toward understanding, and even agreeing with, Husserl's transcendental-constitutive phenomenology, but he would nevertheless draw a line that he did not want to cross—thereby preserving his own realistic intuitions from being overtaken by what he took to be an idealistic philosophy. While thus seeking to understand Husserl, Ingarden also undertook first his famous work *Das Literarische Kunstwerk*,[1] and then the large, carefully argued work on the controversy regarding the existence of the world, *Die Streit um die Existenz der Welt*.[2] One could say that Ingarden's central interest lay in the realism-idealism dispute, and it may also be safely said that no one in the history of philosophy has more carefully analyzed that issue than he. While *Das Literarische Kunstwerk* is deservedly more famous, Ingarden undertook it as much out of his interest in the subject matter of art as out of the desire to advance the discussion of the realism-idealism issue. We shall see how that could be so.

Purely Intentional Objects

A central insight of phenomenology is embodied in the thesis of intentionality: the thesis, namely, that conscious experiences, or acts, are intrinsically directed toward objects. But it is by a series of philosophical moves that transcendental phenomenology appears to invert the thesis, arriving at the conclusion that objects intrinsically refer (in a rather different sense of "refer" from that in the first thesis) back to experiences (actual and possible). Ingarden questions this inversion.

Whereas experiences, or acts, are intentional in the sense of the first thesis, let us mean by an "intentional object" an object that is intended by an intentional act. Thus, when I perceive a thing, the tree out there, for example, is the intentional object of my perception. The same holds good of the objects of thoughts, desires, hopes, love, and hatred as well. Ingarden proceeds to distinguish between "purely intentional objects" and "also intentional objects."[3] The tree that I am perceiving through my window is an *also* intentional object, for its being the intentional object of my perceiving is extrinsic and accidental to it. Besides being a real thing, it is also intentional when some conscious being's intentional act is directed toward it, not otherwise. But a purely intentional object is essentially the target of an intentional act: a meaning (in the sense of a Fregean *Sinn*) is essentially the meaning of a word or of a sentence. A work of art is created by the intentional act or acts of some conscious being. These are purely intentional objects.

Purely intentional objects are furthermore either *originally* purely intentional objects or *derived* purely intentional objects. Purely intentional objects are originally so, in case they derive their existence and their essence directly from the intentional act of some one or other. Derived purely intentional objects owe their existence and their essence to things which themselves, on their part, have borrowed their intentionality, in the long run, from something else. Now a work of art is an originally purely intentional object. But words and sentences possess borrowed intentionality, they derive their intentionality from the intentions of the speakers or users of the language. Their meanings are therefore derived purely intentional objects. Thus, the objects posited by the meanings of the words and sentences of a work of literature—situations, characters, states of affairs—are derived purely intentional objects, they are what they are by virtue of the meanings of the words and the sentences, and the latter again derive their intentionalities from the intentional acts of conscious beings. Thus, there are states of affairs that are objectively existing, and there are states of affairs that are purely intentional objects of the derived sort.

A purely intentional object that is "originally" dependent upon an intentional act is an imagined object, a thought—in general, what Husserl calls a "noema." The being of a noema is dependent upon the being of the intentional act or acts whose noema it is. Such an object, in spite of its purely intentional status, has a certain transcendence, which is not quite the same as the transcendence of a real thing out there in the world.

Keeping these distinctions in mind, we are able to understand why, in Ingarden's view, Husserl, in his transcendental phenomenology, treated the real world as though it were a purely intentional object. In that case, "constitution" amounts to a sort of creation. But did Ingarden correctly understand Husserl? Or, is it the case that in his eagerness to import the realism-idealism issue into phenomenology, he was inadvertently led to a misreading of Husserl?

The Structure of a Literary Work of Art

In order to bring out the force of Ingarden's point, let us briefly draw a sketch of his original account of the structure of a literary work of art. Put very schematically, a literary work consists of: (1) a stratum of linguistic formations: words, sentences, sentence-complexes—the phonetic stratum which has its own value quality; (2) a stratum of meaning-units which themselves are stratified into word-meanings, sentence-meanings, and meanings of higher order sentential complexes; (3) the stratum of represented objects, objects—derived purely intentional objects, that is to say—which are derived from and projected by the units of meanings; and, finally, (4) the stratum of schematized aspects of those objects. Both (1) and (2) are derived purely intentional objects. (2) is derived from the original intentionality of acts of consciousness. The objects represented by the units of meaning are also derived objects, derived from the meaning-units.

It is interesting to note that whereas the original purely intentional objects are accessible to only one consciousness, i.e., the consciousness of the ego who intends them, as they are transformed into words and sentence-meanings, they become intersubjective and get detached from the concrete acts of consciousness.[4]

By "represented objects," Ingarden means everything that is nominally presented: things, persons, occurrences, states, acts, also subjective entities such as characters, visions, emotions, etc. Also to be noted is that assertive sentences (or propositions) within a literary work of art are, according to Ingarden, quasijudgmental; the ontic character of their objects (e.g., of being real things, persons, etc.) undergoes a corresponding modification.[5] The reader is not to regard them however as unreal. The modification of their ontic status is also not quite the same as what Husserl calls "neutrality modification." The modifications are many-layered—something we understand if we remember that within a literary work there are distinctions between the real, the imaginary, and the dream: all these modalities have to be taken as "quasi" forms of the respective, original modalities. Such modifications also affect the space and the time that are represented. The space in which the things, events, and persons in a literary work have their places is neither the unmodified real space, nor the purely imaginary space, nor the ideal geometrical space. The same holds good of time.

Without going into details, I would like to draw attention to one important discovery of Ingarden: this is that the represented objects—including represented space and time—have *spots of indeterminacy*. If the author of a novel has not told the readers about the color of the eyes of a character, we cannot just say—applying the principle of excluded middle—that her eyes must have a determinate color, only that we have not been told what it is and so we just do not know the color. We cannot also say that her eyes have no color. There is rather a spot of indeterminacy in the very constitution of a fictional object, which, as readers, we may be, for ourselves, removing by adding the missing determinations in our imagination. But neither the author nor the reader can fully supply all the determinations *hic et nunc*, which a real individual must have in order to be a real individual. Apart from what the author has said and what follows by implication from what he has said, we cannot say if the individual does or does not possess further determinations. Its constitution is not complete. This should show that real things (in their internal determination) are not like fictional things. Since Ingarden himself drew attention to this, it would be rather surprising if Husserl's theory of constitution of reality followed the model—as Ingarden takes it to be the case—of the "creation" of such derived purely intentional objects as fictional objects.

A few remarks on the stratum of "schematized aspects." Applying Husserl's thesis that an external object is perceived only in some aspect or other, Ingarden comes to regard the role that these schematized aspects play in a literary work as fundamental to enabling the author to vividly portray the represented objects. Images, metaphors, similes are amongst those which enable these schematized aspects to present themselves. These aspects would naturally be different if the objects are external things or if they are "internal" or psychic entities. Although we can never intuitively perceive a fictional object, the author's ability to invoke various aspects can nevertheless succeed in presenting the object to a quasi-intuition.

With this account of the structure of a literary work, we are in a position to return to Ingarden's critique of Husserl. Before we do that, it may be useful to recall his distinction between an artwork and an aesthetic object. The aesthetic object is constituted on the basis of a work of art, but by the reader's or viewer's response to it, in which the work of art is *concretized*, and the aesthetic value qualities which belong to the total work as a work are developed and actualized. The reader or the observer is needed to "interpret" the work and thereby to actualize its potentialities and to complete its constitution. This happens in aesthetic experience, whose essential function is to constitute an aesthetic object.[6] Since there is no one way in which an aesthetic object may be formed, Ingarden asserts the theorem that to every work of art there correspond a limited number of possible aesthetic objects.[7] These possibilities lie not only in the work of art itself, but depend also on the observer as well as on various historical conditions. Thus, even the aesthetic object is not, according to Ingarden, subjective—not subjective in the sense in which pleasure is a subjective state of a person. Even the aesthetic object, in a certain sense, "transcends" the experience of the observer.[8]

Ingarden's Critique of Husserl

The central concern of Ingarden's critique of Husserl is to precisely fix the various senses of "transcendence," and to be able thereby to pinpoint precisely where Husserl makes illegitimate uses of the concept of transcendence. In a letter to Husserl of 1918,[9] Ingarden distinguishes between four senses of transcendence: first, there is the sense in which the meaning of a particular act goes beyond the truly fulfilled content, in which case, the meaning transcends the fulfilling experience; second, and this is a special case of the first, the sense of "reality" of a real thing goes beyond the fulfilling senses of any finite multiplicity of perceptual syntheses; third, for something to be transcendent is to be different from consciousness and its noematic sense; finally, a real entity is transcendent in the sense that its mode of being goes beyond what can be posited in a finite number of experientially evident acts. Further meanings of transcendence, according to Ingarden,[10] are: to be transcendent is not to form a real part of consciousness, and at the same time to be a whole which lies wholly outside of consciousness. If the preceding one is the fifth sense, there is a sixth sense according to which a transcendent object transcends not only acts, but also noemata, so that a transcendent object, in this last sense, contains all its material and formal determinations within itself.

Now, after distinguishing between these senses of transcendence, Ingarden can say that a real thing is not a mere series of perceptual noemata. Husserl's idealistic move consists in first extending consciousness to include meanings or noemata,[11] and then collapse the distinction between real things and such noemata. Both steps, according to Ingarden, are illegitimate. Neither sense-data nor meanings, nor views of things, belong to consciousness, they all are *ich-fremd*.

On Ingarden's view, Husserl first introduced the reduction to avoid the objection raised by Leonard Nelson to the effect that epistemology involves a *petitio principii*.[12] Whether this reading is historically correct cannot be examined here. But the idealist position could never be a logical consequence of reduction. What the reduction could exhibit, or manifest, on Ingarden's interpretation, is an intentional object, a noema, but this procedure does not show that there is no autonomous reality to begin with. Thus, Ingarden distinguishes between "the tree in itself" and "the perceived tree as such." Before the reduction, the tree in itself is presented. Reduction has the consequence that the real tree, i.e., the tree in itself, recedes to the background, while the perceived tree as such comes to the foreground. Thus, the epoché, as a method, predetermines, or rather entails a substantive solution of the problem of the relation of consciousness to the world, rather than leaving open the possibility of other solutions of the problem. A method cannot change the world into a mere phenomenon. The epoché can manifest only an intentional object, not an autonomous reality. This also shows why Ingarden continued to look upon Husserl's transcendental phenomenology as an "idealist dependency creationism" which takes the being of the real world to be heteronomous (i.e., purely intentional, such that its existential foundation lies outside of itself) and derivative (in the sense that real being is being for consciousness) and yet autonomous (in the sense that real things are transcendent in relation to consciousness) as well as existentially dependent on it. Consciousness, for Husserl, is not only sense-conferring, but also productive. "[A]s years passed," Ingarden writes, "Husserl tended in his 'constitutive' investigations to understand this dependence as a certain kind of 'creation' of noematic sense of a certain layer . . . on the basis of the experience of a lower layer."[13]

One of the questions which, on Ingarden's reading, Husserl had to confront is: When is the *Sinn* of a noema *valid*? In other words, a noematic inquiry, which initially brackets the question of reality, had to confront the question of truth, namely the question if the noema under consideration is true or not, if, that is to say, the object of that noema really exists or not. As Ingarden understands Husserl's answer to this question, the object of the noema can be taken to exist, and therefore the noema "valid" or true, when there is a necessity guiding the motivational relation between the founding and the founded noematic layers. That the real existence of the object serves as an index of the necessity of the cognition was recognized by Kant when he wrote: "the object is viewed as that which prevents our modes of knowledge from being haphazard or arbitrary."[14] My perception of the tree in front of me, with its noema "the yonder perceived tree as perceived," is valid—i.e., what I am perceiving is really a tree over there—when the sensory appearances presented to me motivate, not by chance but necessarily, the belief that the appearances are appearances of a tree over there. The question of how to decide that the alleged apprehension of the *Sinn* of an object is a valid apprehension, is what Ingarden calls, following Husserl, "*Konstitutive Rechtsbetrachtung.*" The problem is whether at all from a noematic point of view a criterion for the validity of the cognition can be advanced. Ingarden questions the possibility of such a criterion. Noematic description will be restricted, on his view, to a content that is neutral as to reality and so will never yield the required criterion. The only other alternative, also indicated in Husserl's writings, is that the description will leave everything as it is, which would then yield a trivial thesis.[15]

If Husserl, according to Ingarden, arrived at a thesis that ascribes to pure consciousness a certain creativity with regard to the world ("what is real is nothing but a constituted noematic unity of a special kind of sense which in its being and quality results from a set of experiences of a special kind and is quite impossible without them"), he also recognized that "this creation is, as a matter of fact, not arbitrarily dependent on the wishes or preferences of the perceiving subject. There is an *a priori* lawfulness here which can be disclosed only by a constitutive eidetic inquiry."[16] However, the question still remains whether this eidetic inquiry can yield a criterion of truth, or whether the inquiry would remain at a level of discourse that is indifferent to both truth and falsity. There is a certain justification for this anxiety. I myself have maintained that transcendental phenomenology is concerned with meaning and not with truth.[17] At the same time, one should also bear in mind that phenomenology cannot avoid the question regarding the *meaning* of "truth," and once we have a theory about how the sense "truth" is constituted we must have at the same time a theory about the criterion of truth from within phenomenology's own discourse.

Further Elaboration of These Criticisms

For a detailed development of these criticisms, I will consider Ingarden's Oslo lectures of 1967. In the part of these lectures that has been made accessible in *Analecta Husserliana*, volume 4, Ingarden considers the nature, function, and result of Husserl's reductions. Beginning with the idea of "eidetic reduction," Ingarden draws attention to various phases of Husserl's concept of essence. First, in the second and sixth *Logical Investigations*, Husserl speaks of "species," which is to be understood as an ideal quality which belongs, for example, to two things which are both said to be white, i.e., which are similar in respect to an identical feature (whiteness). In the later publications, the word "essence" appears in the place of "species"; along with "essence" he also uses "eidos." In the *Logical Investigations*, the apprehension of a species was called "ideation." In the *Ideas*, the word "ideation" is generally replaced by "*Wesensschau*" or "*Wesenserschauung*": this is maintained to be a genuinely intuitive act, not an act of thinking. Later on, in a manuscript of 1925 (which is a part of *Erfahrung und Urteil*), Husserl develops the idea of variation as leading to intuition of essences.

The distinction between species and essence is important for Ingarden: the species is an ideal quality shared, for example, by two red things, but what is an essence? Ingarden draws attention to the various things Husserl says about essence in the *Ideas*. First, he tells us that an essence is, to begin with (Husserl says, "*Zunächst*"), the *what* of a thing, i.e., what a thing actually is. Max Scheler calls it *Washeit*, whatness. If the thing is a table, the what is tableness. This what is always something general, but it is as though embodied in this particular thing. Husserl also gives another account of essence, or rather another formulation. An individual object, this table over there, is not only a this-there, but also has a stock of essential predicates which must belong to it in order that other secondary predicates may be true of it. The what in the preceding sense is a component of this latter. The individual thing would change, but it must possess this stock of essential predicates. This essence of an individual thing, according to Ingarden, following Husserl, is also individual; it is what Husserl calls, in the *Ideas*, the essence in its concreteness. Ingarden rightly compares it with Duns Scotus's "Socratitias," the essence of Socrates and of no one else, the completely unique *haeccaetas*. Applied to my consciousness now, this particular experience that I am having now, can we say that it has its own essence? This is a question that certainly should concern phenomenology.

Now, it is true, Ingarden emphasizes, that in the *Logical Investigations* Husserl's theory of essence is realistic. In other words, at this stage of his thinking, essences and other ideal objects are taken to be existing by themselves. Even the first section of the *Ideas* develops such a realistic theory of essence; as a matter of fact, this section was incorporated in the text of the *Ideas* from a much earlier manuscript. Consistently with this realist theory of essences, Husserl also subscribed, at this early stage, to a realistic theory of truth. In the later writings, especially in the *Formal and*

Transcendental Logic, Husserl still speaks of ideal objectivities, but they are now said to have been "instituted" (*gestiftet*). Operations of consciousness, as it were, bring such idealities into being. The distinction between two realms of being, the real and the ideal, which Husserl makes in the *Logical Investigations*, is still maintained in the *Ideas*, although in this latter work reality is idealistically construed (i.e., is said to be merely intentional being), while the ideal entities are still construed realistically. In the *Formal and Transcendental Logic*, the idealistic position is extended also to the ideal entities.

In this move, Ingarden is against Husserl, although unlike the members of the Munich and Göttingen schools he is willing to go along with Husserl's reductions, even with the so-called transcendental reduction, without agreeing with him in the conclusions that Husserl draws from those methodological moves. Let us now turn to Ingarden's discussion of the reductions in the Oslo lectures. When Husserl asks us to put under brackets the "general thesis" about the world—the thesis namely that the world is there—which is constantly implicit in all positing of specific objects, Ingarden questions the very idea that there is such a general thesis. He concedes that there may be moments when one affirms that the world is there. But he questions if there is a general thesis about the world which "potentially" accompanies all our experiences of things in the world. However, Husserl thought that without bracketing, exclusion, or suspension of the general world belief, of the *Urdoxa*, there is no true philosophy. But what precisely is this reduction? We know that it is not doubting the existence of the world, nor is it a denial of the existence of the world. One alternative is to construe it as a sort of "neutrality modification," as in the case of Meinong's *Annahmen*, or as when we consider a proposition without asserting or denying it. Ingarden rejects this construal on the ground that such a neutrality modification alters the original act of positing, whereas Husserl tells us that reduction would not modify the general thesis and that it would only render it inoperative. Another way of understanding reduction is to take it as implying a "splitting of the ego," so that the ego that performs and lives within the general thesis is set apart from the ego that brackets it. Thus, there arise two egos, the "performing" ego and the ego that "stands apart" and "distantiates itself from" the general thesis. Ingarden rejects this understanding in order to save the unity of the ego; it must be possible for one and the same ego to play both the roles. However, in spite of these and many other difficulties in exactly describing the operation of reduction, Ingarden concedes that Husserl was after something important, namely that it is possible to perform what he calls the transcendental reduction. The really pertinent question, however, is whether the reduction accomplishes what

Husserl takes it to do. According to Ingarden, the idealistic sounding conclusions that Husserl draws do not follow from the reduction, but reflect rather his metaphysical prejudgments. Let us see how that could be so. The question he asks is: Does Husserl first develop the reduction and then arrive at his idealistic conclusion, or does he first state his idealism and then develop the reduction? For Ingarden, it is instructive that in the *Ideas* the crucial passages in which transcendental idealism is formulated precede the introduction of the reduction, i.e., the thesis regarding the absolute heterogeneity in essence of consciousness from the world. Ingarden reports that Husserl had responded to this anxiety on his part by stressing that what is stated in the text before the reduction regarding the essence of consciousness and the world is as a matter of fact the result of reduction.[18]

Setting this question aside, Ingarden proceeds to examine reduction much closer. Is reduction an act, a specific act, or is it simultaneously a decision, a resolve ? If it is a specific act that one performs, does this act continue to have its enduring influence on one's consciousness after it has been performed ? Or shall we say that the result of the act is a state of consciousness, a transformation of consciousness? Perhaps we should say it is both an act that one performs possibly repeatedly, and also a state of consciousness that ensues upon such performance. The next question is: When reduction is applied to the general thesis, what does it do? What Husserl seems to suggest is that it is the being-character of the real world and of every thing belonging to the world that would undergo a fundamental modification. Husserl also wants that with the reduction the positive sciences such as physics will remain "excluded." As a matter of fact, the various groups of sciences, the natural, the mental, mathematics, and logic—all these will be "bracketed" along with the general thesis. The same would happen to all material ontologies, also to the existence of God. Ingarden questions this extension of the reduction beyond the general thesis, for he thinks that these sciences, as well as formal ontology, are not committed to the general thesis. To "bracket" all transcendent essence as distinguished from all that is immanent to consciousness is to "bracket" some of those fundamental ontological decisions on which transcendental phenomenology, according to Ingarden, depends. At this point we encounter one of Ingarden's fundamental objections against Husserl—namely, that transcendental phenomenology already presupposes some ontological predecisions. Most importantly, it presupposes an ontology of consciousness, the distinction between the immanence of consciousness and the transcendence of the world, amongst others—without these presuppositions, the reduction cannot even make a beginning. Thus, there is a sort of circularity: one must already know what belongs to the essence of pure consciousness in order to be able to exercise the reduction, and yet it is only the reduction that enables us to apprehend consciousness in its purity.

Ingarden also finds Husserl's overall conception of consciousness problematic. Consciousness, on Husserl's view, consists not only of intentional acts, the noeses, but also of *hyle*. The so-called *Abschattungen*, the profiles of appearances of an object, also belong to consciousness. Ingarden recalls that he had several times asked Husserl whether this patch of red in his visual field belonged to his consciousness.[19] Is it an act? Is it a knowledge of something? Does it have an ego-structure? He recalls Husserl telling him that the sense-datum certainly is not egological. Yet, according to Husserl, a sense-datum, even though it is not egological, nevertheless belongs to consciousness. This entails that on his view, pure consciousness contains acts, sensory data, and unities of meaning (noemata). A unity of meaning is in a certain sense transcendent, and yet it is also a part of my experience. What concerns Ingarden is how these entities, so radically different from each other, nevertheless constitute the unity of consciousness. On Ingarden's view, closer to Brentano's, consciousness is always egological and intentional, i.e., only acts belong to consciousness. If the sense data are *ich-fremd*, one still needs to have an account of their origin. Husserl's idealism could not have a satisfactory answer to this problem. We know how Kant had to say that the sense representations were results of affections by things, and yet how he just could not consistently say that. The problem of the "deduction of sensation" became a crucial issue for German Idealism. It is no less a problem for Husserl, if Ingarden is right.

Did Ingarden Understand Husserl Rightly?

I will now briefly raise some questions regarding Ingarden's criticisms of Husserl and the understanding on which they are based. First, let us consider the problems Ingarden finds in Husserl's concept of consciousness. Ingarden complains that Husserl locates a diverse group of things within consciousness—the ego, the intentional act, the *hyle*, and the noema. There is something right about this complaint, but also something off the mark. The ego is not a content of consciousness. If you take the *Ideas I*, the ego is only an abstract subject pole from which acts of consciousness emanate. As the concrete monadic ego of the fourth *Cartesian Meditation*, the ego is the totality of transcendental life, and, again, not something belonging to consciousness. If consciousness, as transcendentally "reduced," *is* but the correlation between an act and a noema, a temporal occurrence and an atemporal ideal entity, to say that noema belongs to consciousness is misleading, and perhaps false. The act and the meaning, in their correlation—neither taken separately—is transcendental consciousness. In any case, consciousness is not a container or like a sack of potatoes, *within* which you either admit or do not admit entities to have their habitation. Ingarden's persistence to find an answer to questions of the sort "Does *X* belong to consciousness?" is a consequence of his reading Husserl with an eye to the realism—idealism problem, which makes him insensitive to the possibility that perhaps Husserl, by his theory of consciousness, was precisely undercutting that controversy, rendering it impossible to ask that sort of question, and trying to find a way which makes either option pointless. It is with regard to the so-called *hyle*, the *Empfindungsdaten*, that Husserl had to decide where they belong, because of his thesis, in the *Ideas I*, that they are *real* components of the noesis. But this is a thesis that Husserl set aside, recognizing that he was led to it by "sensualistic psychology" (dating from 1930).[20] Even nearly ten years prior to the manuscript from which the just preceding text was taken, Husserl writes that the sensory data are dependent on the thing which is causally related to my *Leib*. The *Dingerscheinung*, he says in this text, has a "*Stempel der Subjecktivität*," but is not subjectivity, nor a part of the ego.[21] We know how Gurwitsch revised this doctrine of the *Ideas I* without in the least giving up Husserl's theory of constitution. So, on this entire issue regarding which sorts of things belong to consciousness, I do not find any merit in Ingarden's objections.

We have reviewed a whole series of objections Ingarden raises against Husserl's transcendental reduction. Is there a general thesis of the sort Husserl wants to "bracket," "neutralize," "suspend"? What sort of act is this reduction? Does the act need to be reperformed again and again? What does it accomplish? Does it not presuppose the very thing it is supposed to accomplish? Does not the epoche imply an "ego-splitting"? Can a method change the world into a phenomenon? Can a method change anything at all? It is indeed misleading to speak of a general *thesis*. A thesis is asserted. The belief in the world is the unasserted horizon, within which everyday beliefs, scientific and religious beliefs arise, are maintained, modified, or rejected. The world is not a totality, for to "bracket" a totality, one must deal with every member of it, and this would be a never-ending task. Again, at the place in the *Ideas* where Husserl introduces the reduction he does speak of the world as a totality. No doubt, again, Husserl's own locution is responsible for misunderstandings, and the exposition of reduction as given in the *Ideas* is far from satisfactory. It is only through reduction that the belief in the world first comes to be recognized as a belief. Before reduction, the world is simply there, taken in its being-there, being-available character. Reduction shows that there is a belief, a taken-for-granted character, a naivete about it. There is thus indeed a transformation, but *not* of the thing (the "tree over there" remains a tree that one can climb, a material, organic entity, and so on, and does not become something else—a shadow, a painted canvas, or whatever else), but of its mode of being. The content remains all that was, its color, texture, height, hardness of the trunk, impenetrability etc.—it remains a tree, no single property of the tree is taken away, save the (naive) existence-claim. But is not that also a transformation? Certainly, but not of the tree, for existence is not a property of that tree just as its color, texture, botanical properties are. "Existence" is a predicate that is the noematic correlate of intentional acts having a certain "thetic" quality. The tree occupies a position in space and endures in time. This having-a-position-in-space-and-in-time is a real feature of the tree and lends it its unique particularity. But "existence" is something else. To say that "X exists" entails minimally that X is an object of belief, and, at the same time, is inserted into (or, belongs to) a specific order—so that the meaning of "existence" varies with regard to these orders (whether X is a number or a material object or a mind), but nevertheless remains identical insofar as the quality of the intentional act must have a commonality (positing belief).[22]

In the transcendental attitude, the existential character is rendered explicit and then "disengaged." Existence is not denied (that would be the case when a [seemingly] presented object is taken to be merely an apparition as in the case of a mirage), it is not doubted (as when I doubt "Is that yonder object a tree or a human being?"). What reduction does, in the words of Gurwitsch, is that "for the sake of arriving at radical and radically justified philosophical knowledge," existential beliefs are not allowed to play any role within the context of phenomenology.[23] Method does not change the nature of things: real trees do not become apparitions. But a method can transform the attitude pervading conscious life. What is transformed is the *Einstellung*. This change of *Einstellung* has radical consequences for phenomenology, nothing for the tree over there.

The *theoretical* character and purpose of reduction is not always clearly kept in mind by critics. Once a theoretical stance is taken, it need not be repeatedly performed. Even if the act is past, its effect is an abiding part of the reflecting ego—unless and until it is subsequently modified or canceled. (If one believes, disbelieves, or is an agnostic with respect to God, for example, one does *not* affirm these attitudes to oneself again and again to be sure that the attitude remains; the position taken remains an abiding part of one's mental life unless and until it is modified or canceled.)

The change takes place with regard to one's consciousness. world now as presented to the transformed consciousness is a structure of noemata. Consciousness *produces* neither the naively posited world nor the world as noema. Each is a correlate of an appropriate *Einstellung*. There is no creation. The charge of *creationism* is an overhasty appropriation of a new mode of thinking to a traditional metaphysical doctrine.

Ingarden moves to the center a question which, in Husserl's thinking, was never assigned that status: this is the question about what Ingarden calls *"Konstitutive Rechtsbetrachtung."* What it concerns is a criterion of the validity of cognition. Since noematic phenomenology, by its very nature, will be neutral as to the reality and existence of the object (of the noema), it cannot yield a criterion by which to ascertain the validity of the claim. "Existence," "reality," "actuality," as I have just said, are *thetic* predicates of the noematic nucleus: they derive from the *quality* of the intentional act whose noema is under consideration, and ascription of such predicates is confirmed by its coherence with the order to which it belongs. For example, if the noema contains the predicate "material object," the thetic predicate " . . . is real" would be confirmed when the noema (and the noesis) coheres with other noemata (and noesis) in which material objects are presented, or the same object is presented from a different perspective. But no such confirmation is final, and any confirmation can be canceled or modified at any time in course of the ongoing process of experience. The "necessity" spoken of by Kant is a formal component of the idea of objectivity, but material truth, in any specific case, depends according to Kant, on coherence with "possible experience"—so also with Husserl.

Essence

If noema is an entity of some sort, what sort of entity it is? In Husserl's ontology, there are just two kinds of entities: those that are *real* and those that are *ideal*. A noema clearly is not a real entity, it is not—as Husserl requires of everything that is real—spatiotemporally individuated. Is it then ideal? If noema is an entity, it must be an ideal entity. An ideal entity is either an essence or belongs to the class of entities Husserl calls "meanings." Is noema an essence?

It is well known that in the first edition of the *Logical Investigations*, Husserl regarded a meaning as an essence (more accurately, as species, i.e., general essence) whose instances are the acts which intend that meaning. In the second edition of that work, and in all subsequent works, he distinguished sharply between meanings and essences. With this latter distinction (which, as a matter of fact, Husserl arrived at in his 1905 logic lectures) in place, and with the "discovery" of the epoché (in 1907), the concept of noema makes its appearance. A noema, instead of being an essence instantiated in the appropriate acts, is rather their correlate. Although Husserl does not call a noema as such a meaning, he does hold that a noema contains within its structure a core that he calls its *Sinn*, which consists of all those predicates that the noesis intends its intentional object as possessing. Thus, if not the full noema (which, as is well known, contains, besides the *Sinn*, other groups of elements), certainly the *Sinn* belonging to it may be called "meaning." In general, Fregean readings of Husserl, especially of the noema, do not take these other elements of the noema into consideration. They take the noematic *Sinn* to be much like the Fregean *Sinn*.

While it is generally accepted by writers on Husserl that a noema is not an essence (a distinction which I have earlier sought to clarify by saying that the concept of essence is an ontological concept, while that of noema is a semantic and a phenomenological one), I want to argue in this essay that there is a sense in which Husserl's earlier position on this matter survives even in the *Ideas* I, a sense in which a noema is an essence instantiated in the appropriate acts.

In order to make out a case for this interpretation, let me begin by giving a very general account of the thesis of intentionality. That every conscious experience has an object toward which it is directed, is a thesis which, if true, should not be controversial. If I have a desire, the desire must be of something. If I have a perceptual consciousness, it must be perception of something. Whoever held that this is not so? How then is the thesis of Husserl to be understood, such that it is both true and controversial?

The sense in which the thesis is noncontroversial would be something like this: there is a thing (event, person, or whatever, maybe even a number, or any other abstract entity, God or an angel) which exists out there; here am I, a real human being, having a conscious experience now; between the two—this experience of mine and that thing there—obtains a *real* connection. The nature of this real connection may be construed in various ways. It is usual to construe it as a causal relation. A causal account is most plausible when the thing to which my experience is so connected is a real thing or event or person. If that thing is an abstract entity such as a number, it is not immediately clear how there may be a causal relation with it. But philosophers' perseverance and imagination have found ways of accommodating such cases. One can be causally related to numerals or to sentences, if not to numbers or to propositions, for example.

There is a standard way of arguing that the causal or any other *real* relation must be different from the intentional relation. The argument is that, even if the object, e.g., of perception, is a cause of the perceptual experience, it is not the only cause, and there is no noncircular way of isolating that cause (from the host of other causes) which is also the object—so that being a cause and being the object (of the same experience), even if extensionally equivalent, are two different properties. This argument may be reinforced by pointing out that when as a young boy I saw a ghost in a cemetery, the object of that seeing was a ghost but the cause must have been some other real thing—e.g., a shadow, in which case, being a cause and being the object fall apart. Dagfinn Føllesdal considers the case of hallucinatory experiences, and setting aside various solutions proposed by the Brentanists, suggests that it is better to characterize intentionality as consciousness's always being *as if* of an object. I will remark on this interpretation of Føllesdal shortly.

Husserl clearly did not regard the thesis of intentionality to be asserting the existence of a real relation between two real things, an experience and a thing out there, but rather of an *essential* structure. In the *Ideas I*, he writes:

> wohl zu beachten ist dabei, dass hier nicht die Rede ist von einer Beziehung zwischen irgendeinem psychologischen Vorkommnis—genannt Erlebnis—und einem anderen realen Dasein—genannt Gegenstand—oder von einer psychologischen und sonstwie realen Verknüpfung, die in objektiver Wirklichkeit zwischen dem einen und anderen stattchatte. Vielmehr ist hier und uberall von rein phänomenologischen Erlebnissen, bzw. von ihrem Wesen die Rede, und von dem, was in ihrem Wesen "a priori," in unbedingter Notwendigkeit beschlossen ist.[1]

It is easy to miss the full force of what Husserl is saying here by reading it in such a way as to find nothing but the general thesis that it belongs essentially to consciousness that it has an object. While Husserl did hold the latter thesis (provided one suitably defines consciousness as he did in the fifth of the *Logical Investigations*), in the paragraph just quoted he is asserting a *distributive* thesis. By this I mean that Husserl is asserting that something belongs to the essence of every specific experience that one may be considering. Take any experience, e.g., my present perception of the tulips in my garden as I am looking through the window. Husserl is asserting that it belongs to the essence of this individual experience that it is the perception of those tulips.

In the first chapter of the *Ideas I*, Husserl not only distinguished between individuals and essences, but held that "to each individual object a state of essential being belongs as its essence."[2] He goes on to define an individual as a this-there whose contentual (*sachhaltiges*) essence is a concretum, i.e., "an absolutely self-sustaining (= independent) essence."[3]

Let us extend this thesis to the particular perceptual experience referred to above. *This* experience—not experiences in general, or perceptions of tulips in general—has its own *sachhaltiges* essence, which we can phenomenologically focus upon. In order to be able to do that, we need to abstract from the question of the existence or nonexistence of those tulips (the latter being a question of a possible true description of my garden this past spring), and from various other contingent features of that individual experience. To the essential structure of this experience as this experience belongs the feature that it is a perception-of-those-tulips. Thus, it is not only an essential truth that consciousness is always of an object and only a contingent truth that I am now perceiving those tulips (I could have been looking in the other direction, thereby seeing instead the house across the street from us); it is also an essential truth that my present perception of those tulips is a perception-of-those-tulips.

Husserl could therefore write:

> Dass ein Erlebnis Bewusstsein von etwas ist, z.B. eine Fiktion des bestimmten Kentauren, aber auch eine Wahrnehmung ihres "daseienden"

Gegenstandes, ein Urteil seines Sachverhaltes, usw., das geht nicht das Erlebnisfaktum in der Welt, speziell im faktischen psychologischen Zusammenhänge an, sondern das reine und in der Ideation als pure Idee erfasste Wesen.[4]

Since each individual experience has its own essential structure to which belongs the being of the object (which happens to be its object), and since this essential structure can be phenomenologically focused upon after the appropriate eidetic reduction, it is not clear where the problem about the so-called objectless acts is. It is only when we think simultaneously from two different standpoints, the natural and the eidetic, that we are led to wonder what must be the experience directed toward when as a matter of fact there is no such thing, and forced to the conclusion that there was no real being-of, only an as-if-of. But once we situate ourselves exclusively in the phenomenological-eidetic attitude, I do not see the force of the point.

One may contend that there are at least two difficulties in making the straightforward being-of (instead of being-as-if-of) the key to understanding Husserl on intentionality. In the first place, the thesis, so formulated, leads one to hold that there are two kinds of objects, some of which exist and some do not, and that is not a very satisfactory position to adopt. Secondly, we need to account for that directedness, to be able to say what that directedness consists in.

As regards the first, it seems to me that the position I have ascribed to Husserl here need not imply that there are two kinds of objects—those that exist and those that do not. If both "existence" and "nonexistence," instead of being predicates of things, are rather thetic predicates within the full noema, being correlates of appropriate acts of belief and disbelief, affirmation and denial, then, strictly phenomenologically (i.e., within the epoché), we can only speak about acts which posit their objects and acts which do not. But are things only taken to exist or taken not to exist? Are there not things that really exist (things such as the Mt. Everest) and things that really do not exist (things such as the Loch Ness monster)? To this, the reply would be that just as the straightforward predicates "existence" and "nonexistence" are correlates of appropriate doxic acts, so are the modified predicates "real existence" and "real nonexistence" correlates of corresponding modified acts of confirmation and disconfirmation. There is no way we can return to the prephenomenological account of things, and revise our understanding of intentionality in that light. The only path left for us is just the reverse.

As regards the second objection, it is right that the task of phenomenology is to account for intentionality, to describe its structure—this task is not eliminated by taking intentionality to be straightforward directedness, nor is the task any more pertinently pressing if we say it is "as-if-of." In either case, saying what intentionality is, is only the beginning of philosophizing about it.

If Husserl throws light on what intentional directedness consists in or tries to account for that directedness, can we further ask: Just what is he after? What does "accounting for" here mean? What does "consisting" mean?

On one account, determining what the directedness just consists in is to show by phenomenological analysis that

$$1.\ \text{the act} \longrightarrow \text{object}$$

should be expanded into

$$2.\ \text{hyle} + \text{noesis} \longrightarrow \text{noema} \longrightarrow \text{object}$$

I perceive those tulips. That this perception of mine is perception of those tulips in just the way they are perceived, from this perspective, under that description, belongs to the very essence of this particular perceptual experience. It would be a mistake, therefore, to suppose that it needs to be accounted for why this perception is perception of those tulips. For it is not as though there is the perception here (in me) and the tulips out there, and we want to know how this perception comes to be about those flowers. This question cannot be asked, for this perception is, in its essence, perception-of-those-tulips. You don't have an indeterminate perception which, then by some means, gets around to be of those flowers. To think, then, that this trick is done by or through the noema is misleading, to say the least.

It is only from within a naturalistic standpoint, possibly, that such a question—misleading and perhaps impossible to ask from within the epoché—can be asked, and answered. The question that is asked within the naturalistic standpoint is different from what we tried to ask. That question then would be: How do those flowers make me perceive them? By stimulating my sensory receptors, so the story is likely to begin.

Within the epoché, we can neither ask, how is it the case that my perception is of that object? Nor can we ask the naturalistic question, how does that object produce in me this experience?

What question is left for the phenomenologist to ask, in answering which he will account for the intentional directedness? We need to replace the broad act-object schema by the fine-grained schema, by more and more fine-grained structures. More fine-grained than the schema (2) is possible as soon as we bring in the consideration that both hyle and noesis are temporal processes within the phenomenologically lived inner time-consciousness.

If what I have said is true, then *hyle* should not be understood in terms of sensory inputs or sensory receptors, as a matter of fact, in any causal language such as "the present impingements upon my sensory surfaces." The causal story, or the causal half of the story, is quite legitimate, but just cannot take off the ground within the epoché. Thus writes Husserl: "Hyletische Daten sind Farbendaten, Schmerzdaten, usw. rein subjektiv betrachtet, also hier ohne an die Leibesorgane und an Psychophysische zu denken."[5]

The noema then belongs to the essence of a specific experience. But it is still not an act's *own* essence, for there are conceivably other acts having the same noema. In order to get to the essence of *this* act and of no other, one may have to insert into the noema such features as the temporal stretch and position of the act, which as a matter of fact Husserl tries in a rather puzzling text.[6]

The purpose of this chapter has been to highlight the fact that even after the emergence of the concept of noema essentialism is not abandoned. To the contrary, the noema itself is understood both as the meaning-correlate of the noetic act as well as the act's essence.

However, it would be still misleading, perhaps false, to find in the noema the essence of the object—a mistake one finds too often in the literature. Being a mode of presentation, a noema, by itself, does not guarantee that it truly presents the essence of its object. It is through a coherent system of noemata that the essence may be said to come to givenness.

6

Transcendental Philosophy and Lifeworld

A Note about the Meaning of "Transcendental"

After Kant and Husserl, it is surprising that it should be necessary to distinguish between "transcendent" and "transcendental." And yet many authors, and especially critics of transcendental philosophy, mistake the transcendental for the transcendent. So it would be helpful to reiterate at the beginning that the domain of the transcendental is not one that transcends the empirical, lies beyond it, raised high above it, belonging to a Platonic realm of supersensuous realities. It is rather that which constitutes, and thereby renders the empirical possible.

However, to this last statement, we need to add a note. While it is usual to contrast the transcendental with the empirical, *that* is *not* the fundamental contrast, whether for Kant or for Husserl. Not for Kant, because for him the transcendental is the a priori condition of the possibility of empirical cognition as well as of synthetic a priori knowledge (in mathematics and in physics). Consequently, the transcendental (pertaining to the a priori constitution of the faculties of sensibility and understanding) explains how any cognition (empirical as well as a priori) is possible. In Husserl's thinking, the basic contrast is between the constitut*ing* and the constitut*ed*: to the latter belong material objects as much as cultural objects, individuals as much as essences, numbers as much as logical forms. Nothing that is constituted is transcendental. The transcendental is the life of consciousness, intrinsically intentional and temporal, meaning-conferring and synthesizing, objectivating and interpreting.

If the fundamental contrast is *not* between the transcendental and the empirical (for both Kant and Husserl), it would be mistaken from the perspective of Husserlian phenomenology to claim that the transcendental is a priori. If all a priori is not transcendental (the mathematical a priori, e.g., is not), neither is the transcendental a priori. Thus, the transcendental ego as such is not an *eidos*, although one can speak of the *eidos* "transcendental ego." A transcendental ego is an actual ego with its own transcendentally purified (through epoché) stream of experience, in which case the locution "transcendental experience" has an undeniable legitimacy.

Two Senses of "Subjectivity"

For the purpose of bringing out the full power of transcendental thinking, it is necessary to distinguish between a narrow and a wide sense of the constitut*ing* domain. In the narrow sense, it is the domain of consciousness; in the wider sense, it is the domain of subjectivity. Obviously, for my present purpose, "subjectivity" has a wider extension than "consciousness."[1] Consciousness is a subset of the domain of subjectivity, and—as a consequence—not all subjectivity is consciousness. Thus, e.g., bodily subjectivity—the subjectivity of "oriented" movement—is not consciousness. What characterizes the entire domain of subjectivity is intentionality, but all intentionality is not intentionality of an act. Even the unconscious which presumably inhabits and underlies consciousness is not physical, but rather subjective unconscious, consisting in unconscious intentionalities. These distinctions need to be kept in mind if we are to be able to evaluate the rather too often advanced claims that the corporeality of the self as also the presence of the unconscious in the heart of consciousness militate against transcendental philosophy. They limit the power of consciousness, but do not affect the constitutive scope of subjectivity. The Kantian categories are constitutive forms of consciousness, just as the Kantian forms of intuition and schematism via imagination are operations of subjectivity that fall outside the limits of consciousness. The constituting, and so transcendental domain, in Husserl's philosophy, is subjectivity, and not restricted to consciousness.

Two Senses of "Essence"

It is also necessary to be clear about the logical relation between transcendental philosophy and essentialism. More often than not, it is taken for granted that a transcendental philosophy is essentialistic. While this larger question will not be discussed in this essay, it is a prerequisite for a discussion of this question that we be clear as to what "essence" could mean in the context of transcendental philosophy. There is a certain prima facie opposition between essentialism and transcendental philosophy, inasmuch as the former lends support to a dogmatic ontology (and a dogmatic epistemology of intuition, of eidetic intuition in this case), and the latter generates the spirit of critical overcoming of any ontology and dissolution of any provisional givenness by exposing their hidden, anonymous constitution. But, at the same time, since a theory of transcendental constitution can only *begin* with what is already constitut*ed*, or rather with its *sense*, it cannot afford to indulge in that seemingly radical critique which begins by "suspecting" that very constituted sense. Consequently, a certain kind of essentialism is not only compatible with, but goes with transcendental philosophy. For such an essentialism, the *essence* is constitut*ed*, has had a history, and thus in Hegel's sense, has come about, "*was gewesen ist.*" At the same time, being tied to the idea of meaning (*Sinn*), the essence becomes relativized to a certain perspective and hovers in between a purely *de re* and a purely *de dicto* construction. What is essential and what is accidental to an entity are thereby relativized to the perspective of the investigator, to the meaning one assigns to that entity. The two conceptions of essence I have in mind are then: the classical, which is based on separating the invariant features from amongst the total content of a thing; and the phenomenological, which results from "transforming" every content of the *what* of a thing into an essence by detaching it from its existence here and now.

Two Forms of Transcendental Philosophy

We can now introduce the important distinction between a transcendental philosophy—à la Kant—which investigates into the a priori conditions of the possibility of a given body of *truths* such as (in Kant's case) Euclidean geometry and Newtonian physics, and a transcendental philosophy—à la Husserl—which, not committed to any such privileged body of truths, would inquire into the constitutive conditions and origin of any such theory regarded as a *meaning*-structure (its truth-claim suspended), as well as into the constitution of the prescientific perceptual world. With this difference in the nature of the tasks undertaken, the two conceptions of transcendental subjectivity also differ. In the Kantian sort of philosophy, the transcendental constitutive source is a pure, nonempirical, also ahistorical formal consciousness, whose structure corresponds to the categorial features of Newtonian mathematical physics. In the

Husserlian sort of philosophy, the constituting subjectivity is concrete, sensuous-hyletic and also intentionally meaning-bestowing, corporeal and also historically developing, anonymously constituting and also reflectively discovering its operations. It is this latter sort of transcendental philosophy, with its idea of a concrete constituting subjectivity, which is the concern of this essay. This constituting domain is transcendental in the second of the two senses of "transcendental" distinguished above; it is "essential" in the second of the two above mentioned senses; it is "subjectivity" in the second of the two defined senses.

The Transcendental-Empirical Distinction

As distinguished from the Kantian philosophy, for a phenomenological transcendental philosophy, transcendental subjectivity and empirical subjectivity do not form two distinct domains, but are one and the same life of consciousness considered from two different perspectives. Considered as a part of nature, as subject to the laws (especially causal laws) of nature, as belonging to a natural entity (i.e., to a physical, biological, and psychic being called "man") in whom it is caused by external and internal causal conditions, it is empirical. Considered as that through which nature receives its meaning as "material," "biological," or "psychic" being, which provides the access to all that is, but for whose internal structure no world as a world (i.e., as an organized whole of objects) could be presented, subjectivity is transcendental. "Being natural" (or a part or a product of nature) is an interpretation of subjectivity by itself, but as the source of this, indeed of any such interpretation (both of itself and of its world), it is transcendental. This way of distinguishing the two applies to every component or layer of subjectivity. The body, observed from outside and thematized by objective sciences, is a natural entity. The same body, as lived from within, as felt and experienced by itself, is transcendentally subjective, inasmuch as its intentions and intentional movements and projects confer meaning upon the surrounding world as well as upon itself.

Construed in this manner, the understanding of transcendental subjectivity as the form-giver—with the associated picture of someone (the putative transcendental ego) who legislates from above—needs to be abandoned. Conscious life is not a chaotic disarray of sensations, but always meaningful intending of objects belonging to a world, and this intending is made possible by consciousness's own inherent structures through which multiplicities are unified at every level. There need be no absolutely rock-bottom givens and no absolutely empty forms. Sensations emerge as organized into perception of objects; perceptions of objects emerge against the background of a larger horizon; impulses and desires are organized in meaningful goal-directed actions, and actions as exhibiting a character, a character as characterizing a whole life. These organizations exhibit principles of organization and categories of meaningfulness. To say that they are unified by an ego, a self, a subject, is to say no more than that these principles and categories constitute experience as it grows and develops. The putative ego itself is a unity that comes about as a result of modes of synthesis inherent in a conscious life.

Regarding the empirical-transcendental distinction, I have elsewhere advanced three claims.[2] First, I have claimed that transcendental subjectivity is *ontologically* prior to the empirical-causal order. I have also claimed that the life of consciousness, *in itself*, is not mundane but transcendental. I have also maintained that the *concept* of transcendental subjectivity has superior explanatory power. Against these three claims, David Carr has raised the following criticisms.[3] Carr argues, in the first place, that *only if* the empirical-causal order is considered as a meaning-structure (this antecedent is not his but mine) then it must be traced back to its constitutive origin in the transcendental, as all meanings must be. But this conclusion follows only from a certain way of looking at the empirical-causal order, not otherwise. Secondly, my contention that it is phenomenological reduction that shows consciousness to be, in itself, transcendental, begs the issues, for the reduction presupposes a prior decision not to consider consciousness as mundane. Thirdly, since the physicalist and the existentialist can have a place in their schemes for intentional meaning-bestowing acts (i.e., they can explain these latter *in their own terms*, if not, to be sure, in terms of transcendental constitution), the claim I make to the effect that "transcendental subjectivity" has greater and more comprehensive explanatory power must be mistaken. The consequence seems to be that the universality-claim of the transcendental philosopher is as much based on his prior decision, as is the universality-claim of the physicalist.

Carr's first argument implies that the transcendental philosopher must have to show that the empirical-causal order is a meaning-structure. I believe this is what both Kant and Husserl show, in their own different ways though, and I need not here repeat their arguments. However, if such an argument is admitted as being reasonably plausible, it would seem one cannot stop there. One must be willing to admit that even the transcendental structures—including the transcendental subjectivity itself—are no less meaning-structures. I have, at various places, conceded that the talk of transcendentality itself is an interpretation taken over from the history of Western thought. In that case, the truly transcendental is that which is the source even of this interpretation, the source of all interpretations—the historically developing life of the spirit (to use a Hegelian locution). Carr's second argument rests upon the question: What could possibly motivate the transcendental reduction? If reduction is to open for us access to the transcendental domain, the reduction has to be motivated from within the mundane order. This question has been discussed in the literature at length, and such commentators as Fink and Landgrebe have taken part in the discussion. There are three sorts of answers that are suggested. First, reduction is totally unmotivated, in exercising reduction the philosopher is exercising his freedom not to participate in the beliefs of the natural standpoint. The second sort of answer is that reduction is motivated by one of many possible mundane motives—for example, the idea of philosophy as first science or the idea of providing foundation for all cognition, these ideas being available from the history of human thought. The third sort of response insists on a certain ambiguity in the entire situation: in the natural attitude, reduction appears completely unmotivated, in a philosophical attitude which seeks to understand the natural attitude, it finds sustenance in the historically available ideas of first science and foundational cognition, but the true sense of reduction emerges only at the end and not at the beginning. The charge of begging the issue has to be examined in the light of these three possibilities, but while doing so one needs also to bear in mind that the reduction is *not* a method to isolate a new domain of being—Husserl's misleading locutions to that effect notwithstanding—but to understand our experiencing-of-the-world in its inmost nature as meaning-bestowing and constitutive of the world.

At this point, Carr's third worry confronts us. Why should what reduction lays bare be regarded as the *inmost* nature of our experience-of-the-world? At most, this is just another way of looking at things. How can one establish the superiority of this way of looking over the many others—the physicalist, the psychologistic, or the existential? The point I have sought to make is that the physicalist, e.g., has no plausible account of the meaning—bestowing function of intentionality, whereas the transcendental philosopher has an explanation of physics. Let me, however, further elaborate this contention. The physicalist's explanation of intentionality would not only relegate intentionality to a phenomenal status, but would, in the long run, *refuse* to find a place for it in the scheme of things as envisioned in physicalism. He would refuse to do so not because he is hard-headed, and were he more liberal he could admit intentionality into his scheme, but because the scheme itself has no place for it. So his explanation of intentionality has to culminate in a rejection of the explicandum. Now, consider the other possibility: the transcendental philosopher explains physics by assigning to it a phenomenal status (as did Kant) and/or giving an account of the interpretive acts that go into the constitution of physics as a theory (which would involve an account of the constitution of logic, pure mathematics, measurement theory, and something like Husserl's account of Galilean physics in the *Crisis*). He may have to go beyond this, and have an account of what more, beyond physics, is involved in physicalism. But in no case need he reject them as simply false. He would have done so, if he had his own ontology, his own preferred picture of the world, e.g., a sort of panpsychism or an idealistic metaphysics. But since he abjures all ontologies as constituted theories, he need not have to say that physics or physicalism is simply false. This is what I meant when I said that the transcendental point of view has superior, more comprehensive, explanatory power.

Carr states the problem in a manner that makes it appear almost insoluble: "Perhaps, they [the physicalist and the existentialist] cannot *account* for these acts in transcendental-phenomenological terms; but then that is not their job. Science provides causal accounts and existentialism provides existential accounts. To ask them to provide transcendental accounts would be like asking phenomenology to give causal or existential accounts." Carr recognizes that I do not want this to be so. The impossibility of phenomenology's giving a causal account or of physics's giving a constitutive account is trivial. In comparing the two points of view, I was obviously not asking: Who, of the two, can do *both* the jobs, or who (of all possible points of view) can take over the jobs of all the rest? I was asking: Who, of the two, can have an account of the possibility of the other's *theory* without simply rejecting it as false?

Carr also raises the question, which would seem to be unavoidable for philosophy: Which one, the transcendental subjectivity or empirical subjectivity, is the real me? Am I, my true self, an intentional, meaning-giving, nature- and world-constituting being, or am I a natural, causally conditioned being? Note that the questions, "Am I embodied or not?" Am I historical or ahistorical?" are, at this level, not decisive questions, for, as I have argued elsewhere[4] and as phenomenology recognized, contrary to the philosophical tradition, transcendental subjectivity is historical and corporeal as well. So the truly decisive question rather is: If "transcendental" and "empirical-natural" are two ways of considering the same thing, namely, my conscious life or life of consciousness, what is this life of consciousness (within which my sense of my own "I" is constituted) in itself? Is it one or the other, or is it neither?

My contention is that transcendental philosophy need not make a metaphysical assertion as to what my self is. It can show only the priority of the transcendental perspective, insofar as it can critically reflect upon its other, the natural; but, one could also say that the transcendental presupposes the natural as the *given*, already available, upon which to reflect. Furthermore, transcendental philosophy cannot answer the question "what is the mode of being of transcendental subjectivity?" (a question that was posed for Husserl by Heidegger), because the very sense of "being," of "reality," or even of "really real" would have transcendental explications or constitutive origin. The transcendental, then, has to be located beyond being and nonbeing, beyond any ontology.

Alternately, if one wants to construct a metaphysics of the self on the basis of transcendental phenomenology, one may construe the transcendental as a possibility of self-reflection, self-critique, self-understanding, and self-legitimation—a possibility which defines me as a thinking, rational being. Such a possibility of rational selfhood may then be regarded as *founded upon* a *given* experiential and existential basis of facthood, in which case one can speak of "layers of selfhood" rather than of *the* real self. But to develop such a thesis is beyond the scope of this paper.

Transcendental Philosophy and the Lifeworld

One of Husserl's great achievements was to sketch the possibilities of transcendental reflection to its outermost limits, in order to encompass within its scope what always resisted its domination—namely, the everyday, concrete, world or the lifeworld. This is in sharp contrast to the classical transcendental philosophy, which was a philosophy of science, and dealt with perception (Kant's synthetic a posteriori judgment) only insofar as perception was incipient physics or the perceptual world was also the world of physics. It should be recognized, however, that Kant, of whom the above characterization is true, went beyond the limits of philosophy of science when he thematized, in his third critique, nature as it is the object of aesthetic and teleological judgments.[5]

Husserl's thematization of the lifeworld should not be read as a radical departure from his earlier mode of thinking. On the contrary, its avowed aim is to overcome a naïveté of classical transcendental philosophy by making explicit an unacknowledged presupposition—the presupposition of the lifeworld as the forgotten "foundation of sense" for physics and mathematics. Husserl's efforts in the *Crisis* consist not only in bringing to light this forgotten foundation of modern science, but also in pushing through questions regarding the transcendental constitution of the lifeworld itself. First, there is the question as to how the sciences arise from the lifeworld. While the general answer to this is indicated by the world "idealization," a detailed execution of the solution would involve how idealization works in the case of the mathematical sciences, how idealization is involved in the application of mathematics to the experienced world, and also how idealization, in the form of empirical typification, works in the social and human sciences.

In addition to this, and more fundamental than this, there is the transcendental question, concerning what sort of intentionalities operate in the constitution of the lifeworld itself—a question which itself may consist in various layers of questioning, not to speak of the equivocation of the very concept of the lifeworld as between the perceived world and the cultural world, the latter being explicitly historical, the former containing an ahistorical core, even if we grant that the way things are perceived, their perceptual meanings, are culturally and so historically conditioned.

In view of the possibility of such questionings it would be mistaken to regard the lifeworld as a foundation beyond and behind which it is impossible to penetrate. It is therefore ironic that many antifoundationalists would stop at the world of everyday praxis as the ultimate foundation for all theoretical enquiry.

Practice, Praxis and Transcendental Questioning

The lifeworld is a world of *practice* (of action, making and doing) and *praxis* (of social action, of production of goods, exchange of goods, and distribution of goods). It would, however, be mistaken to say that these modes of *acting* exhaust the lifeworld in all its dimensions. For example, there are religious, aesthetic, and ethical dimensions. By virtue of these, the world as well as things in the world are presented to subjects inhabiting that world with different sorts of values—as useful, as sacred, as beautiful—all of which can be brought under the general heading "cultural." It would be also a mistake to hold that the lifeworld is not a *cognitively* apprehended world, or that things in the lifeworld are not *objects* of cognition but are simply acted upon and evaluated. It is perhaps plausible to hold that the cognition that we have within the lifeworld is not yet the highly idealized form of cognition that is exemplified in the natural sciences or in mathematicized and also philosophical disciplines. But cognition there is—as much as practice and praxis and valuation. There is a core of perceptual cognition at the heart of the experience of the lifeworld—a perceptual cognition that is inextricably linked with action and evaluation. It would be a mistake to say that such cognition and action present things, events, persons, and situations in their unique individuality, as *this-there* in their *hic et nunc,* and then to draw the consequence that such unique individuality cannot be "reconstructed," "retrieved" within philosophy. A rather naive example of such skeptical questioning is the well-known challenge made by one Herr Krug to Hegel, asking him if he could deduce the pen with which he was writing from the categories of his logic.

As against such a skepticism, I will make the following remarks: Things are cognized, acted upon, evaluated not only as unique individuals, but also, simultaneously, as exemplifying *types.* The this-here-now goes together with the "this-here-now ø," where ø stands for a type. Furthermore, there is no ground for holding a romantic theory of action, according which action brings one into contact—unmediated contact—with brute reality (whereas cognition, especially theoretical cognition, removes you from that immediacy irremediably). Action and praxis present the world to the agent *as having a certain meaning,* they too have their *Sinne,* they too exhibit, to reflective glance, a noetic-noematic structure. The world is interpreted as much by the purely theoretical cognizer as by the practical agent. If that be so, transcendental questioning cannot be resisted even with regard to the lifeworld.

One can begin with questions about the possibility of the perceptual world, with its horizonal and temporal structure, its intersubjectivity and historicity. One can go on to ask how perceptual meanings are derived from practical orientation, from the mobility of the body, as well as from the cultural tradition that is taken over. One can ask how the meanings derived from a cultural tradition succeed in "overlaying" and "clothing" the world. Needless to say, transcendental questionings at this level are not as precise and clearcut as at the level of the idealized scientific cognition, but their messiness reflects the messiness of the categories of lifeworld. We would still be looking for the modes of subjective (even if bodily, à la Merleau-Ponty) intentionalities which constitute the lifeworld; we would be, in such investigations, involved in doing a transcendental philosophy of deeper levels—of levels beneath the Kantian. We may have to be in search of Freudian unconscious intentionalities, Jungian collective unconscious, even Derridean traces (freed from the manipulations by the overpowering *Différance*). We shall be pursuing the Kantian program, encapsulated in Hermann Cohen's epigram: "*Nichts ist gegeben, alles ist aufgegeben.*" I would slightly change it to say: "Everything that is given, opens up new tasks (*Aufgaben*) to be solved." In this sense transcendental philosophy is critical and rejects any dogmatism, including the dogmatism of the lifeworld. The result, on the positive side, is that we progressively retrieve a more profound picture of the constituting transcendental subjectivity.

7

On Derrida's Reading of Husserl

Derrida is a master reader, and has heightened our critical awareness of reading a text. He has also been seriously concerned with Husserl's philosophy, and has produced some fine readings as well as interpretive commentaries (and deep critiques) of Husserl's texts. But has he *read* Husserl correctly? Some of his criticisms of Husserl, as is unavoidable, presuppose the validity of his reading. It is therefore imperative that we look carefully at the latter. Such a project may require that one also keeps in mind any general theory of reading that Derrida may have. But I will not, for the purposes of this lecture, undertake to expound and critique that theory, and will prefer to go directly to Derrida in relation to Husserl texts. I will not also be directly concerned with Derrida's various criticisms and his deconstruction of Husserl; however, to the extent such criticisms and deconstruction rest on his understanding of Husserl, they would unavoidably be affected by our evaluation of that understanding. Although Derrida originally develops some of his own philosophical concepts in the context of his reading and critique of Husserl, they are not dependent on that reading and that critique—so that even if Derrida's understanding of Husserl is found to be seriously flawed, it would by no means follow that his own philosophy must therefore be rejected. But if his deconstruction of Husserl fails, then one may be led to suspect whether or not all such deconstructions rest upon a reading (deliberately or not) made to suit those deconstructive projects. But if deconstruction is a mode of reading that suspicion may be unfounded, and if deconstruction seems to rest upon a reading made to serve that purpose, that is precisely as it should be. For in that case, there would not be two things—a reading and then deconstruction—but one move: namely, a deconstructive reading, which may then be *judged* as a reading. All these questions will be untouched in this essay.

Let me recall, however, that Derrida often speaks of, in his context of reading Husserl, a "reading that can be neither simple commentary nor simple interpretation."[1] As we all know, that is more often than not the case with *all* reading, so that the fact that one is always staking a middle ground need not bother us, for we just cannot do anything else.

The Tradition of Husserl Scholarship

Before Derrida came on the scene, there had already developed a distinctive line of Husserl interpretation in Belgium and France by men such as G. Berger, J. P. Sartre, M. Merleau-Ponty, A. De Waehlens, E. Lévinas, and P. Ricoeur. In all these, leaving Berger aside (who wrote the first major essay on Husserl in French, and who was more inclined toward a Cartesian than an existential reading), the influence of Heidegger was decisive in the formation of the picture, in varying degrees and forms, of an existential Husserl. Consequently, certain general features allow themselves to stand out: a rejection of "transcendental reduction," an underplaying of Husserl's *Logical Investigations*, an injection of the hermeneutic standpoint into the reading and critique of Husserl, and a critique of Husserl's so-called "theoretical" prejudice—including Merleau-Ponty's priority of "operative" intentionalities over the so-called act-intentionalities; Lévinas's critique of Husserl's prejudice in favor of the theoretical; and Ricoeur's prioritization of the will and reading of intentionality as being basically voluntaristic, and his recognition of the centrality of history (à la Hegel and Marx) and historicity (à la Heidegger) to the Husserlian doctrine of constitution. In this reading and critique of Husserl, Hegel and Marx, as seen through Heidegger, and as expounded by Kojève and Hyppolite, played a dominant role. Nevertheless, i.e., despite these mediations, the ideas of subjectivity, intentionality, meaning-constitution, and "lived time" retained their unquestionably Husserlian ancestry. The result became what may be called an "anthropological reading" of Husserl.

This peculiar French reading stood in sharp contrast to the two schools of German Husserlians: the earlier "realist" phenomenologists who, inspired by Husserl's Göttingen program of eidetic research, retain the essentialism and correlative intuitionism of Husserl's so-called "realistic" period; and the transcendentalists, who took the alleged "idealistic turn" of Husserl, according to which all meanings, including the meaning of the world and of others are constituted within the life of the transcendental ego.

There is also a common point of view, taken over unquestioningly by a successive generation of Husserl scholars, which divides Husserl's thinking career into several well-demarcated phases marked by radical breaks and conversions (allegedly in response to external challenges). Briefly put, the account runs like this: as a student of Brentano, Husserl began as a "psychologistic" philosopher of mathematics; Frege's highly critical review of his first published work, *Philosophie der Arithmetik*, led Husserl to abandon that psychologism in favor of an objectivistic and Platonist theory of essences and meanings (and a concept of "pure logic"); the Neo-Kantian influences of Paul Natorp led to a "reversal" of this realistic position into an idealism (a return to the earlier psychologism with the addendum that now he was speaking of transcendental subjectivity, not the maligned psychological) of a sort (now called transcendental-phenomenological idealism); and, finally (again, allegedly, as a response to the challenge of the growing influence of Heidegger's thought), this transcendental idealism was abandoned in favor of a return to the thesis of the primacy of the *Lebenswelt*, the lived intersubjective world.

I do not wish to give reasons, in this essay, why I consider this account of the development of Husserl's thought—this story about ruptures and reversals—mistaken. But it is against the background of this varied tradition of Husserl scholarship—to which may be added the linguistic and analytic Husserl interpretation pursued in this country by such philosophers as Føllesdal and his students, Jaakko Hintikka, and this author—that I want to place Derrida's reading of Husserl, so that we can appreciate the novelty as well as the frailty of that attempt.

Some Features of Derrida's Reading of Husserl

Derrida's reading of Husserl, when considered in the light of the above summary account of the traditions of Husserl scholarship, is remarkably daring. Insisting as he does, and rightly in my view, on the continuity of Husserl's thought (and so, by implication rejecting the above-sketched story of the development of Husserl's thought), Derrida begins by focusing *first* on Husserl's last major essay ("The Origin of Geometry") and on the opening sections of his first volume of the *Logical Investigations* (separated by a period of thirty-six years). By taking the *Logical Investigations* seriously, as being central to Husserl's thought, such that the *Ideas* not only does not contradict the *Logical Investigations* but "continuously clarifies it,"[2] Derrida stands apart from the tradition of Husserl scholarship formed in France. (In this judgment, I will make an exception in the case of Ricoeur who, in developing his account of the relation between phenomenology and hermeneutics, always returns to the first volume of the *Logical Investigations.*) Neither is Derrida, unlike his French predecessors, a critic of Husserl's transcendental move. On the contrary, in an important sense, he carried Husserl's transcendental reduction to its *supposedly* logical consequence.[3] Furthermore, his interest in the *Logical Investigations* is not confined to the theory of meaning; he takes Husserl's idea of a "pure logical grammar" most seriously, and claims to free it from the constraints Husserl supposedly placed on it.[4]

Since he believes in the continuity of Husserl's thought, he may be said to read—as Barry Smith, a dear friend, complained of me—the earlier work of Husserl in the light of the later. In other words, he reads the very opening paragraphs of the first of the *Logical Investigations* as containing a phenomenological reduction (whereas not until 1905 did Husserl on his own account discover the reduction recorded in the so-called Seefelder manuscripts).

Convinced though he was of the inseparability of transcendental thinking from Husserl's early philosophy of meaning and logic (in a review of my *Edmund Husserl's Theory of Meaning* of 1964, Derrida had taken me to task for having tried to do this "illegitimate and impracticable" task of separating the philosophy of meaning from the transcendental problematic),[5] and though he may be regarded in one way as having radicalized Husserl's reductions, he was not yet quite free from the influence of Merleau-Ponty's thesis that a complete reduction is not possible. Derrida writes: "As soon as it is admitted that autoaffection is the condition for self-presence, no pure transcendental reduction is possible," and adds: "But it was necessary to pass through the transcendental reduction in order to grasp [this]."[6]

But just as the thesis of continuity in Husserl's case saves us from the dangers of positing imagined ruptures (neglecting the lessons to be drawn from the mass of manuscripts left behind and now being available), that thesis should be correctly understood, for otherwise in finding the latter thesis in the earlier works one misses the point that continuity does not mean absence of any new discoveries and certainly not the possibility of *deepening* of the problems and solutions as are to be found in the earlier works.[7]

In another respect, Derrida remains within the tradition by modifying the primacy of the theoretical, and construes—not unlike Ricoeur—intentionality as being in essence voluntaristic,[8] Husserl's *Bedeutung* as "wanting to say" (*vouloir-dire*),[9] and transcendental phenomenology as "transcendental voluntarism."[10]

However, what is most important is that Derrida unequivocally rejects the anthropological reading of Husserl (as also of the other two: Hegel and Heidegger) espoused by Kojève. Wasn't the critique of anthropologism one of the initial motives of Husserl's thinking?[11] This critique concerns not only empirical anthropologism, but also transcendental anthropologism. The transcendental subjectivity of Husserl is not what the French existential phenomenologists called "human reality." Derrida rejects a similar anthropological reading, in postwar France, of Heidegger's analytic of *Dasein*. Neither Husserl nor Heidegger was an anthropologistic thinker, although Husserl, on Derrida's view, "precipitously interpreted *Sein und Zeit* as an anthropologistic deviation from transcendental phenomenology."[12] Since I am not, in this chapter, concerned with Derrida's reading of Heidegger, I will not comment on this last issue. But I will suggest that one good place we should look at, in order to think if Heidegger's thinking in *Sein and Zeit* was not a sort of anthropologism as Husserl had complained, is the "correspondence" between the two in connection with Husserl's article on phenomenology for the *Encyclopaedia Britannica*.[13]

Derrida on Some Fundamental Husserlian Concepts

After these general remarks, I will focus, in this essay, on Derrida's interpretations of some of the fundamental Husserlian concepts. These are: intentionality, ideality, expression and meaning, and time.

First, as to intentionality: Husserl's position regarding intentionality, as developed in the *Logical Investigations* and the *Ideas*, amounts to the following structure:

$$\text{Ego} \longrightarrow \text{hyle} + \text{noetic act} \longrightarrow \text{noema} \longrightarrow \text{object}$$

For Derrida's general remarks on intentionality, I will depend on his *Limited Inc*, as well as on *Speech and Phenomena*. It is not true that Derrida rejects intentionality; what he rejects is the priority, the universal legislative power, of intentionality. This last claim is what he questions, always drawing upon Husserlian resources. Doesn't Husserl say that the intentional directedness of an act does not logically entail that the object toward which it is directed must be a real entity? "It makes no difference whether the object exists or is fictitious or even impossible."[14] At the same time, the telos of intentionality—construed voluntaristically—is total "fulfillment, realization and actualization." But such total fulfillment is, in no case, possible—as Husserl himself well recognizes. Thus, by its very nature, intentionality is doomed to failure, and so strives in vain to actualize itself. There is necessarily a *presumption* that the intention will be fulfilled, but this is no more than a presumption. Even the very possibility of frustration, of nonfulfillment—to take a weaker claim—belongs *structurally* to the essence of intentionality. Derrida calls it "possibility qua necessity."[15] Thus, starting with Husserl, Derrida argues, one can see that Husserl both recognizes this presumptive character of the claim to fulfillment, and yet is still committed to the possibility of fulfillment. And yet, just as Merleau-Ponty had said that "the absolute positing of a single object is the death of consciousness,"[16] so Derrida asks: Isn't the pure realization of self-presence, the presence of a fulfilled and completely actualized intention, itself also death?[17]

The other aspect of intentionality is the noema or the ideal meaning, which is an ideal object. A large part of Derrida's thinking about Husserl concerns the constitution of an ideal object. Ideality, so says Derrida, drawing upon Husserl, is "the correlate of a possibility of indefinite repetition."[18] But, again, at this point, Husserl's texts exhibit a paradoxical feature. On the one hand, ideality is constituted by pure repetition, and yet, on the other, the ideal object is present, is intuited, is given, in the living present.[19] Infinite repeatability implies endless postponement, deferral. Constitution of meaning, of ideality, is never complete. Note that Derrida is not saying that constitution of new meanings is always going on, he is rather saying that no ideality ever gets constituted, for that would involve an endless process of repetition. So much is a part of his reading of Husserl, but Derrida himself goes beyond this, and argues that iteration, repetition, involves difference (besides identity), *the same* is identified in and through differences, so that each constituted identity is split from within by differences.

Let us proceed further. Husserl's intentional act, belonging to an ego, perishes, but the meaning, the ideal noema, remains. Thus, both the subject and the object may be absent without affecting the ideality of the meaning (and also of the text, i.e., the linguistic ideality). If that is so, then like the possible absence of the object, also the possible death of the subject, "structurally" and necessarily, belongs to the nature of the ideal object. To quote Derrida, "the purportedly ideal structure must necessarily be such that this corruption will be 'always possible.'"[20]

There is another aspect of the Husserlian theory of intentionality which Derrida takes most seriously: this is the thesis that every intentionality has a horizonal character, which means that all intending is in a given context. The horizon consists of determinate features and further determinable features, anticipated in generalities more or less emptily, to be filled in as one progresses in one's explorations. But the context, once recognized (as it was by Husserl), cannot be kept within limits. It is never exhaustively determinable, it "is always, and always has been, a work *within* the plan and not only around it."[21] It is also always "transformative-transformable, exportative-exportable."[22] As a matter of fact, Derrida says that one of the definitions of "deconstruction" is "the effort to take the limitless context into account; and thus to an incessant movement of recontextualization."[23] Given such possibilities of "recontextualization," such "limitlessness" of context, identity, identification, and total idealization are not possible: an "essential nontotalization" holds good.

This leads me back to Derrida's early concern with Husserl's concept of sign.

The first of Husserl's six *Logical Investigations* begins with a distinction between two kinds of signs: signs that are merely indications, and those that are expressions of meaning. Every sign, however, is sign for something: this is its generic feature which, Derrida complains, Husserl never gives. Every sign, no matter if it is an indicator or an expression, is a sign for something: that indeed is its generic feature. A generic feature is always to be found along with specific features. Being a sign for something can be either in the mode of an indication (in which case, in the first place, there is a lack of insight into the relation between the sign and the signified, the relation being one of "motivation" bred by association, and, in the second place, the sign as an *existent* entity motivates belief in the *existence* of the signified) or in the mode of an expression (in which case what is *expressed* is a *sense*, or a thought). After drawing this distinction, Husserl distinguishes between *not* two kinds of expressions, but two roles that expressions may play, or rather two contexts in which they may function—i.e., in monologue and in dialogue. This change of function has nothing to do with whatever makes an expression an expression. What Husserl does is a kind of eidetic variation, in order to bring out what is invariant in both contexts. What is invariant is expression of a *sense*—which constitutes the essence of an expression qua expression. Another function that an expression performs when uttered by a speaker in a communicative situation is what Husserl calls "intimation" (*Kundgebung*). The speaker's utterance intimates to the hearer what mental experiences the speaker is having (believing, doubting, questioning, ordering, etc.). Clearly, in monologue, the speaker and the hearer being the same, this intimation is redundant. Moreover, while in communication, an actual production of the physical word (in speech or in writing) is needed, in monologue the words are merely imagined and not perceived as existent. What we have is an "imaginative production of the word." But that the word does not actually exist, but is only imagined (not perceived), does not interest us. Hence, the monologue is a case of pure expression, for the function of expression is not here mixed up, contaminated, polluted by the other function of intimation.

Derrida finds here several decisive steps—and these findings are intertwined with a way of reading Husserl. Note that the question is not whether Husserl's emphasis on monologue or soliloquy, in order to let the essence of expressions show itself, is a step in the right direction or not. The question rather is: why did Husserl take this step, to what purpose and how does this questionable step hang together with his later moves such as epoché and transcendental phenomenology?

The thesis of the priority of writing over speaking is extended by Derrida to his work on Husserl's 1936 essay "The Origin of Geometry."[24] Note that Husserl already speaks of "the origin of geometry" in *Philosophie der Arithmetik*.[25] Geometry as an ideal structure is constituted not only by the inner acts of thinking by the geometrician, by his creative mental activities, but by language, through which, as Husserl writes, "it receives, so to speak, its linguistic living body" (*Sprachleib*).[26] For what Husserl there calls "the *persisting existence*" of the "ideal objects," what is needed is *written documentation*, which makes communication possible "without immediate or mediate personal address."[27] "[W]riting-down effects a transformation of the original mode of being of the meaning-structure."[28] Derrida finds here a confirmation of his thesis that the constitution of idealities needs— contrary to the claim of transcendental phenomenology—"written texts," "documentation," i.e., recording in sensible, empirical, material signs. At the same time, Husserl recognizes the importance of history—of a new sort of history—for phenomenology: the history of the constitution of ideal objects, of meanings, which constitutes a tradition. Derrida sees in this new concept of history a departure from the "historicist empiricism" of Dilthey (does he understand Dilthey correctly at this point?), and understands Husserl as avoiding "the philosophical nonsense of . . . empiricism." But, as in the case of "sign" (where he asks about the meaning of "sign in general"), so also here he asks: what is the "*unitary ground*" which makes the distinction between factual history and intentional history possible? (as he will also ask later: What is the *unitary meaning* of "life" which makes the distinction between empirical life and transcendental life possible?). Thus, as always, Derrida sees Husserl's phenomenology "stretched between the finitizing consciousness of its principle (i.e., evidence as the immediate presence of the thing itself "in person" and *now*) and the *infinitizing* consciousness of its final *institution*, the goal being indefinitely postponed, deferred in its content but always evident in its regulative value."[29]

Some Critical Remarks

Who here is the metaphysician? Husserl or Derrida? Without answering this question, let me make a series of remarks touching upon the points

Derrida raises in course of his reading of Husserl. Again, let me repeat: Derrida may be right in his criticisms of Husserl's views, but for me the question is: Does he rightly interpret Husserl?

1. First, as to sign in general: "indication" (or indicating, *Anzeichen*) is *not*, for Husserl, the genus of "expression."[30] Nor is indication a coordinate species (along with "expression") coming under the genus "sign": for, if it were so, then an expression could not also function as an indication (in communicative speech). The unity of "sign" (as comprehending indications and expressions) is not a generic unity. The unitary meaning of "sign" is "to stand for something." But the sense in which an indicative sign stands for something and the sense in which an expressive sign stands for something are radically different senses of "standing for." The common notion of "standing for" is rather an analogical notion, not a generic one. To say, as Derrida does, that Husserl does not tell us what sign in general is, is to *presuppose* mistakenly that, on Husserl's view, "sign in general" is a generic notion.

2. Husserl's consideration of monologue, before determining the essence of expressions, is *misleading* inasmuch as expressions are expressions insofar as they express publicly sharable ideal—but *not private*—meanings. It is *not* the case that monological expressions alone are *pure* expressions and that expressions functioning in dialogue are impure. The case of monologue only serves to bring into operation an eidetic variation, bringing to light the eidetic fact that expressions, to be expressions, must *express* meanings—no matter whether they also serve as indications or not. If triangles, in order to be triangles, need not be right angled, or be of any specific dimension, that does not entail that any specific or a right-angled triangle is not a pure triangle. It is not also true, as Derrida supposes, that with the transition to monological speech, Husserl reduces empirical worldly existence,[31] that we have Husserl's transcendental reduction already in operation, that the existence of the world is not implied, or that the imagined word is a noema. All of these are based upon misreading Husserl's text. On Husserl's view, the only function that drops out of operation is *Kundgebung*, or intimation of the speaker's mental states to the auditor. The function of referring to the world remains, as does also the mundaneity of the act of inner speaking or imagining (which just because it is not publicly heard or seen does not become transcendental). The ideal meaning, on Husserl's theory, is the correlate also of the empirical consciousness, not only of the transcendentally reduced one.

3. What then about the alleged priority of writing over speech? On Husserl's own view, the production of ideal meanings does not require inscriptions, but the constitution of a science *as a tradition* to be inherited by

succeeding generations requires the production of written texts. Derrida need not have found this recognition in as late a text as "The Origin of Geometry." Already, in the early *Philosophie der Arithmetik*, Husserl writes:

> Das es eine wichtige Aufgabe der Wissenschaft wäre, sich mit scheinbar so untergeordneten Dinge zu beschäftigen, als es die Wahl sinnlicher Zeichen ist, dürfte im ersten Augenblicke Bedenken erregen; . . . wir werden sogleich sehen, wie der Unterschied zwischen Wort- und Schrift-Zeichen für die Arithmetik so wesentlich ist, dass eine notwendige Beschränkung auf die ersteren eine erheblichere Entwicklung der Arithmetik zur Unmöglichkeit gemacht hätte."[32]

Husserl continues to say that it is even important whether one writes with pen and ink on paper or on a dusty tablet with a stick—which can influence the progress of arithmetical method. Then he asks, should not this be a part of the logical method? I will not here ask if in holding this view Husserl as well as Derrida is right. But Derrida, to my mind, confirms Husserl's own early view, and not one against him.

4. One of Derrida's more powerful, and often repeated, criticisms of Husserl, which makes use of a certain reading of the texts, concerns the relation between ideality (of meanings, noemata, and of essences) and repeatability. Husserl certainly held that the ideal entity is repeatable, it is not a unique occurrence—which would make it real (and, so, temporal). However, Derrida misleadingly reads Husserl's position to be that ideality is *constituted* by repeatability, by the "and so on endlessly" (*immer weiter*) of the process of repetition. From this reading, it becomes for him an easy step to argue that this endless repetition both (1) endlessly postpones (defers) the constitution of idealities, and (2) introduces a difference into the texture of an ideal entity's very being (for every repetition is different from every other). I must point out that Husserl's view regarding the constitution of idealities is, however, quite different. In order to bring that out briefly, I must distinguish between constitution of physical objects and constitution of idealities. A physical object—more accurately, the sense "physical object"—is constituted by the possibility of perceiving (visually and tactually, at the least) the same object from different perspectives. This possibility is never exhausted, since for Husserl the sense "physical object" has a presumptive character about it. Derrida, unfortunately, reads Husserl's texts about ideality in the same manner. However, an ideality is constituted not by an endless series of actual and possible repetitions, but by and in the very act in which it is grasped. If the ideality is a meaning, it is constituted by the act of intending/grasping it; if it is an essence, it is constituted by this act of eidetic intuition resulting from the

process of eidetic variation. An ideal entity is repeatable. Repeatability is a mark of ideality, not what makes it ideal. And what is more important—and Derrida misses the point altogether—is that we should *not* construe "repeatability" *nominalistically* or extensionally as a never-ending succession of particular acts of reiteration,[33] but *eidetically* as *essential possibility* of iteration. The nominalistically construed series cannot be brought to an end, but the *essential possibility* of iteration is grasped in one single act of iteration *of the same*. It is a nominalistically conceived idea of repeatability as an endless succession of particular acts of repetition which sustains Derrida's thesis that constitution is bound to be perpetually "deferred." For Husserl, there is then no such deferral.

If, however, "repeatability" is construed as "imaginability of repetition," then Derrida's argument seems to rely upon the fact that imagination refers to perception. Thus, he writes: "[Imagination] retains a primary reference to a primordial presentation, that is, to a perception and positing of existence, to a belief in general."[34] This argument again is misleading, and certainly does not prove what it is meant to.

5. These remarks lead to two of Derrida's most powerful interpretation-cum-critiques of Husserl. One concerns Husserl's privileging of "presence," the other frees intentionality from both the subject and the presence of the object. In each case, it is difficult to separate Derrida's reading of Husserl from his critique of Husserl. Taken as a reading, the first one is more correct, the second simply is off the mark. It is undoubtedly true that in spite of his "opening up" the present, the now, to the just elapsed past (by retention) and the just-about-to-come future (by protention), the *now* remains the center of the retention-protention structure, so that even if no object is merely now, my awareness, my flowing experience is always passing through, and at any point of time, is a now phase. If Heidegger's analysis of time privileged the future, Husserl's privileged the present—even if the present is a "spacious present." Privileging the present, however, need not imply either adequacy or apodicticity of what is given. Thus, even if Husserl considerably modified his earlier claims to adequate and apodictic cognition, the primacy of the present (although surrounded by a horizon of absences, even of an absence, the just past, that is present to retention) remains. *In this sense*, he is logocentric, but whether logocentrism is a disease, a failure, an illusion to be gotten rid of or a philosophical strength, a virtue, an insight to be preserved, has to be decided on other independent grounds. My own preference is for the latter alternative.

6. The misconstrual of "repeatability" that I have pointed out has its counterpart in a misconstrual of Husserl's ideal of "genesis." Derrida rightly emphasizes, even in his first work (on Husserl) only now published,

that the idea of "genesis" is central to Husserl's thinking. But Husserl's own understanding of genesis must be read *together with* his structuralist-essentialist position, and not in opposition to it. Derrida recognizes that even in his structuralist phase, Husserl does not reject all genesis but only that which is causal and naturalistic.[35] Distinguishing between three directions Husserl's later genetic phenomenology takes—the logical (in *Experience and Judgment* and *Formal and Transcendental Logic*), the ego-logical (in *Cartesian Meditations*) and the historical-teleological (in the *Crisis*)—Derrida follows the last of these as leading to a metaphysics of history, so that he could conclude that the result of phenomenology is metaphysics. In view of this *critique*—but not refutation—of Husserl, I will, briefly though for this chapter, take a look at Husserl's conceptions of history and genetic phenomenology.

Although Husserl did sometimes speak about factual history or the history of the historians, and *always* rejected historicism (insofar as "historicism" is understood in terms of factual history), what he develops in the *Crisis* is not a theory of *that* history, nor does he ever come to accept the historicism he had earlier rejected, notably in the *Logos* essay.[36] The history he now begins to make room for is (1) intentional history understood as genesis of sedimentation of meanings; (2) this genesis can be retrieved not in terms of factual historical research,[37] but rather within the reflecting ego's own "reduced" mental life (as Husserl does in the case of the genesis of modern physics); (3) this history requires, not a Heracleitean conception of flux, but a theory of identity of meanings so that the constitut*ed* meanings are again and again available; (4) it is also inseparable from the inner time consciousness of the ego in communion with other egos, so that the intentional history is the history of a community. Husserl's history then is not even a mundane history of ideas; it is rather a transcendental history of subjectivity, insofar as this subjectivity is already communal. As Husserl writes in the *Crisis*, it is "nichts anderes als die lebendige Bewegung des Miteinander und Ineinander von ursprünglicher Sinnbildung und Sinnsedimentierung."[38] This historical process is teleologically directed toward rationality, toward *Vernunft*. The "inner history," Husserl writes, "necessarily leads further to the already explained highest question regarding a universal teleology of reason."[39] It is this last thesis which is so much likely to be misunderstood. We cannot correctly interpret Husserl at this point unless and until we correctly understand what he means by "reason," and what sort of "teleology" he wants to maintain.

Husserl's idea of *Vernunft*, despite his use of words such as "absolute," has *nothing* to do with a metaphysical idea of *Vernunft* as an absolute reality which stands behind, and expresses itself in and through, history and nature. For Husserl, the idea of *Venunft* is connected with (1) absolutely *grounded* truth-in-itself; (2) the idea of the thing that is presented as being self-given in adequate and apodictic evidence appropriate to the sense of that thing; and (3) the idea of reason as belonging to the essence of a human person. From (2) it follows that *Vernunft*, for Husserl, should not be identified with intellect; a thing may be self-given in sensory experience, through bodily kinaesthetic experiences and through passive synthesis. In any case, the idea of adequate and apodictic self-givenness remains an infinite idea. It is such rational knowledge, and the consequent rational ethical self-responsibility which is the telos of "intentional history."

Derrida rightly emphasizes that Husserl is concerned not with the external history of facts, but with the *inner* history,[40] that he reduces empirical history to this "pure" history,[41] that all historicism, according to Husserl, remains at the level of factual history, that the universal *a priori* of history is the "inner historicity" of the ego in its intersubjectivity,[42] and that this historicity—which is the same as the universal and essential structure of transcendental subjectivity—is itself *Vernunft* or reason, so that "reason" should not be construed as a human faculty.[43]

To show the nature of Derrida's interpretation of Husserl's understanding of "history" and "historicity," let me recall another, more recent, commentator's interpretation of the same. Elisabeth Ströker insists[44] that the question of transcendental-phenomenological genesis is not a genuinely historical question, that Husserl's concern is not *when* the constitutive achievement in question came about, but *how*, that Husserl had not found a point of access to genuine history, that Husserl's sense-history was history so-to-speak, which explains why Husserl speaks of "history" always in quotation marks, and that although Husserl carried out much of his investigation pertaining to history in close connection with the analysis of time, he never attended to the specific structure of historical time.[45] Husserl inquired into depth-problems quite unknown to ordinary history[46]—working back through the manifold *layers* of sense formations.[47] This inner history, according to Ströker, is "in principle nothing but intentional analysis pursued to the point of complete exhaustion of its methodological possibilities as intentional history."[48]

In this last quotation, Ströker points to the limits of phenomenology. Not unlike her, Derrida also sees in Husserl's late thinking an attempt to radicalize phenomenology up to a point where phenomenology encounters its own limit. This happens when eidetic phenomenology returns to come to terms with a transcendental *fact* (as distinguished from the transcendent, constitut*ed* fact),[49] where the distinction between outer and inner is obliterated, where the finiteness of phenomenological evidence yields room to the infinity of a Kantian Idea, i.e., the idea of endless determinability of being. These are all perfectly sound readings of Husserl, and have been noted by many writers on Husserl not particularly interested in Derridean deconstruction.

If Husserl's late writings exhibit metaphysical pronouncements, that is not because phenomenology turns—by an internal negation—into metaphysics. It is because Husserl always recognized that phenomenology was not coextensive with philosophy and that phenomenology left room for metaphysics, by which he meant not a concern with "naive and inconsistent ideas of things in themselves," but all concern with contingencies of the facticity of life and death and questions about the "meaning" of history.[50] It has been mistakenly maintained that Husserl's constitution analysis looks for an apodictic grounding of the world. On the contrary, the constituting transcendental subjectivity is not apodictic in any meaningful sense. The *fact* of constituting subjectivity, the absolute being, the *Urfaktum*, is possibly a metaphysical concept, but marks a point where the metaphysics is transcendental—phenomenological.

Concluding Remarks

Derrida's understanding of Husserl, as we find it in his introduction to "The Origin of Geometry," is in my view as "Husserlian" as that of any other. One does not expect all interpreters of a philosopher—especially of a philosopher as complex as Husserl—to agree in their interpretations. Derrida's is a viable interpretation, faithful to the texts, aware of the enormous complexities of Husserl's thinking, and willing to understand rather than to refute. However, as the "deconstructive" project grows and takes over, and clichés such as "logocentrism" and "metaphysics of presence" dominate the critique, the remarks on Husserl tend to lose that original faithfulness. In no case, however, should Derrida be read as having attempted a refutation of Husserl. For American Derrideans who have unthinkingly taken over those clichés, and who have too hastily taken Derrida to be refuting (or, better still "deconstructing") Husserl, a text from Derrida, dating from 1985, is worth quoting. The text occurs in the context of a commentary on Apel. Derrida refers to his own work as "ein wirkungsvolles und vielleicht unbeendbares Hindurchgehen durch die transzendentale Phänomenologie Husserls."[51] Rejecting the charge that he is a relativist or historicist, Derrida continues: "Was mich betrifft, so habe ich zu sehr meine Muttermilch an der Brust der transzendentalen Phänomenologie eingesogen, die zunächst eine rigorose Kritik des Relativismus, des Psychologismus, des Empirismus, des Skeptizismus und des

Historizismus war, um gegen diese Quasi-Dämonen nicht gefeit zu sein." He goes on to say that his deconstruction of Husserl "ist von mir immer mit der Ermahnung versehen worden, die transzendentale Dimension eines Denkens der spur zu berücksichtigen, das keine Semiotik mehr, aber auch nicht die Rückkehr zu einem prätranszendentalen Empirismus wäre."[52]

8

Foucault as a Philosopher

Although Foucault has often said that his work is not in the discipline called "philosophy" ("of the universities," he would add), it has been generally claimed that some of his theses, if true, must be of considerable importance for philosophy. This is indeed as it should be, for being the sort of discipline that philosophy is, it cannot but be stirred by new ideas in any other science, be it natural or social/human. But in Foucault's case, there are special difficulties in claiming large philosophical significance for his work, and I shall begin by drawing attention to some of these in the first part of this chapter. In the second and the third parts, I will focus on a couple of theses of Foucault, which are as such philosophical and of great importance, no matter if they are in the long run acceptable or not.

The Philosophical Significance of Foucault's Historical Studies

> I have never had the intention of doing a general history of the human sciences, or a critique of the possibility of the sciences in general.[1]

Foucault celebrates the rise of specific revolutionary movements as contrasted with the global ones, and also of specific intellectuals.[2] His own scientific work has been in connection with certain specific conflicts—notably, those in medicine, psychiatry, and penal systems. The idea of large universal histories and of universal revolutions are, in his mind, connected with the conception of philosophy as a universal discipline, i.e., a discipline which allegedly provides all human knowledge and action with a foundation, purpose, and meaning. The question that I want to ask, first, is: If we take Foucault on his own words, i.e., if we take him as a specific intellectual abjuring philosophy as a discipline, what philosophical significance could his work nevertheless have? I will not

77

even attempt to call into question the validity of his specific historical work in medicine, psychiatry, and penal systems. Assuming their validity (or truth in the only sense admissible by Foucault, i.e., in the sense in which "truth" is not separable from "power"), one still would want to be clear about their bearings on philosophy. Clearly, there are several possibilities to choose from: (1) one may hold that works such as Foucault's in such specific areas need have no bearing on philosophy; (2) one may concede that the bearings they may have on philosophy need be of no greater significance than the vast changes in the natural sciences in this half of the century; or (3) one may contend that despite Foucault's denial that he was doing philosophy, his work cannot but have profound influence on philosophy. Let us consider these three possible views.

1. The first view is that Foucault's work in such specific areas as history of medicine, psychiatry, and penal systems, like any work in the empirical sciences, can at best only underdetermine philosophy. Work in these areas can be of momentous importance for the social sciences, but philosophy is not a social science, although it may have the social sciences, or at least some aspects of them, as its subject matter. By augmenting/modifying what philosophy has to think about, work in the social sciences and in history may indirectly influence philosophy, but it cannot by itself determine what shape philosophy will take. It can do so as little as developments in quantum mechanics or discoveries of the DNA structure can by themselves force a change of course of philosophy, except by way of providing philosophy with interesting results to focus upon. If observational data underdetermine the sciences, the scientific theories on their part underdetermine philosophy. For example, the methods of writing history have been changing, new methodologies are being pressed, and new looks are being taken at the past. These changes in the nature of what historians do have affected the nature of history as a science—but not the nature of philosophy in general. They may at best provide grounds for a new philosophy of history, in the same way as quantum mechanics provides the basis for a new philosophy of physics that radically departs from the philosophies based on classical physics. But that distinction is within philosophy conceived in a certain manner—it does not entail a radical departure in the very nature, conception and role of philosophy.

2. This brings us to the second view, which concedes that Foucault's fascinating historical studies should provide new problems for philosophical thinking, and necessitate revisions of some marginal concepts, especially in philosophy of the social sciences or perhaps in philosophy of history—but none of these changes need be more radical than those occasioned or necessitated by many sea changes taking place in the

sciences today. So why specifically focus on Foucault? The only reason his pioneering and in some respects revolutionary work may seem to be of greater philosophical import than many other pioneering and revolutionary work in biology, genetics, and the information sciences is that philosophy may be regarded as in a certain sense *closer* to the concerns of the social/human sciences than to the natural sciences. But this last is a questionable assumption. If we reject this assumption and hold that philosophy is neither a social/human science nor a natural science, but is a mode of thinking which derives some of its subject matter from all those sciences equally, then there is no reason why Foucault's specific historical studies should have any more importance for philosophy than work in those other fields. Such a position is perfectly consistent with his disclaimer that he was doing philosophy, though it would leave most philosophers dissatisfied. They would prefer the third alternative, and insist that his researches do profoundly affect philosophy in a manner in which researches in physics and the life sciences do not. Let us see how a case can be made for such a view.

3. To appreciate Foucault's importance for philosophy, one needs to bear in mind the state of philosophy that prevailed in France up until the sixties. That state of philosophy may best be described as a confluence of the ideas of the three H's: Hegel, Husserl, and Heidegger, culminating in the existential phenomenologies of Sartre and Merleau-Ponty. To Husserl, it owed the idea of transcendental subjectivity as constitutive of all mundane objectivities. To Heidegger, it owed the centrality of *Dasein* as being-in-the-world, being characterized by a hermeneutic preunderstanding of itself and its world and by historicity and temporality, which make the Husserlian transcendental-constitutive role unattainable. To Hegel, it owed a conception of subjectivity as developing through history toward a comprehensive self-knowledge, or rather of history as a process through which spirit progressively comes to know itself. The key concepts and concerns of this era were: subjectivity, constitution, temporality, and history. Foucault's researches may then be seen as contributing to the destruction of the centrality of the nexus of these concepts. This is achieved (a) by developing a theory of how subjectivity itself is constituted; (b) by offering a theory of constitution of domain of objects by discourse; (c) by rejecting the priority of time, especially of the inner, lived, experiential and existential time; (d) by highlighting discontinuity (of episteme, of events, of discourses), which makes it impossible for reflection to appropriate all history into its own thinking; and, finally, (e) by rejecting the classical philosophical idea of "truth" in favor of one that is inseparable from "power." If these are amongst the results of Foucault's researches, it would seem to be undeniable that they seriously affect philosophy—

but only if they are the results of Foucault's researches. But are they? I suspect it can be shown that they are not. They are rather results of *philosophically* interpreting certain interesting "historical contents"[3] or "a solid body of historical fact"[4] discovered and juxtaposed by him. If that is the case, what we would have on hand is not a case of historical researches exposing philosophy's pretensions, but rather a less interesting case of a certain philosophical interpretation claiming to set aside another on the basis of allegedly factual discoveries. Such a position would still be able to sustain (3), but would render this alternative much less significant.

In order to render my case regarding (3) plausible, but not securely established, let me consider several theses Foucault advances regarding "power." My purpose, I repeat, is simply to draw attention to the *nature* of these theses.

The Concept of "Power"

> [And] for all that I may like to say "I'm not a philosopher, nonetheless if my concern is with truth then I am still a philosopher.[5]

> Power is neither given, nor exchanged, nor recovered, but rather exercised and . . . it only exists in action[6]

> [The] individual is not a pre-given entity which is seized on by the exercise of power. The individual, with his identity and characteristics, is the product of a relation of power.[7]

> Power must be analyzed as something which circulates. . . . It is never localized here or there. . . . Power is employed and exercised through a net-like organization.[8]

> Truth isn't outside power, or lacking in power. . . . truth isn't the reward of free spirits, the child of protracted solitude, not the privilege of those who have succeeded in liberating themselves. Truth is a thing of this world: it is produced only by virtue of multiple forms of constraint.[9]

> It seems to me that power *is* "always already there," that one is never outside it, that there are no "margins" for those who break with the system to gamble in. . . . Power is co-extensive with the social body.[10]

> Its success is proportional to its ability to hide its own mechanisms. . . . For it, secrecy is not in the nature of an abuse; it is indispensable to its operation.[11]

Now, what kind of concept is this concept of power? I want to suggest that, though clearly not the same, it is very much similar to the sort of concept that the Hegelian concept of *Geist* is. The Hegelian *Geist* is always with us, beside us. As a matter of fact, we are in its midst. This is what Hegel says in the context of his critique of Kantian epistemology in the Introduction to the *Phenomenology*.[12] Spirit is not a thing, a substance, "a lifeless essence," but "actual" as intersubjective, in the community (which is a network of relationships). It exists, we can say, in action. The individual, in his modernistic individuality is constituted, not pregiven: in this constitution, i.e., in the constitution of self-conscious subjectivity, desire, need for recognition, and conflict are necessary moments. Human desire is desire whose object is not a thing, but another desire (recall that, for Foucault, power is action directed to other actions); but the mode of operation of *Geist* is not restricted to exploitation, domination, and repression. *Geist* is also synthesizing and harmonizing—not to be sure, presupposing consent (as power also, for Foucault, does not). The operations of *Geist* are multifarious, irreducible to any single type. *Geist*, as is well known, is what it is through its other. It faces nature as an alien power. The oppositions between consciousness and the unconscious, the known and the unknown, truth and subjectivity, one's own and what is alien, self-consciousness and nature—all these belong to the life of the *Geist*. Clearly enough, I have the conception of *Geist* of the *Phenomenology* in mind, freed from the optimism of reaching absolute knowledge, i.e., of *Geist* as process and freed from a linear conception of history. Perhaps there is only one major impediment for thus construing the Hegelian *Geist*: the Foucauldian thesis of discontinuities, breaks and ruptures which prevent us from talking about one historical process realizing a plan of the *Geist*. I will return to this idea of discontinuity later in this essay. For the present, it needs to be emphasized (a) that the history of the spirit, according to the *Phenomenology*, is a series of shapes whose distinctions are not intended to be obliterated even with absolute knowledge; (b) that these shapes are, in an important sense, discontinuous (although Hegel thought there is a logically necessitated transition from one to its successor, the sense of *this* necessity is never quite clear, and a certain contingency persists about the series); (c) that they all do not line up as succeeding each other in linear time, for that succession does not quite correspond to the actual history; and, finally, (d) that a certain circularity characterizes the life of the spirit as a whole as well as each phase of it. If we keep this complicated picture in mind, and also recall that the familiar dialectical triad (with a synthesis of opposites) does not fit all Hegelian movements (as Croce, Müller, and Findlay, amongst others, have well pointed out)—then a certain formal affinity between Foucault's *power* and Hegel's *Geist* becomes apparent, despite his claims to have left Hegel on the way side. Add to all this the

Hegelian "cunning of the Reason": Foucault's power also succeeds by "hiding its own mechanism."

The way Foucault saw his relationship to Hegel (having studied with Hyppolite) is best expressed in a telling passage which shows his awareness of: "the extent to which Hegel, insidiously perhaps, is close to us . . . to which our anti-Hegelianism is possibly one of his tricks directed against us, at the end of which he stands motionless, waiting for us."[13]

Let me reiterate that my purpose, in this section, is *not* to show how much of a Hegelian Foucault was. It is intended to emphasize that Foucault's fundamental concepts, such as that of power, are basically *philosophical* concepts—in the case of power, a *speculative* concept—not naturalistic or scientific ones, that the perceptions that Foucault abandoned philosophy to do positive science in search of facts (and documents) or that he radicalized "naturalization" of philosophy[14] are just mistaken. No positive science of fact can lead to *the sort of thesis* he arrived at (the thesis, namely, that knowledge and power are inseparable). The so-called genealogy is a philosophical thesis that goes beyond any science and in fact is not the result of any scientific discovery. Being a philosophical thesis, it needs to be freed from the pretense of scientificity and to be examined as such. To say, as Foucault said, that the concept of power he put forward was nominalistic, that power is how it works, distributed along the different centers of power—and not unified in a point of origin, such as the state, the sovereign, or God—would not make the thesis any less philosophical: nominalism is a philosophical, not a scientific theory by virtue of its pretended positivity and scientificity. As a matter of fact, the Hegelian *Geist* is no less distributive—synchronically and diachronically. One could very well say that *Geist* is how it works. Hegel's discourse, one may add, is more honest in the sense that from the very beginning it abandons the positivist notion of fact, making the notions of facthood, objectivity, and truth relative to each "shape" of the spirit—thus leaving no neutral observation data against which to measure the large philosophical thesis about "spirit." Foucault remains ambivalent on this score.

"Subjectivity" and "Constitution"

It is not power but the subject which is the general theme of my research.[15]

There are three philosophical theses advanced by Foucault to which I now wish to draw attention, in order to reflect on them and bring out their significance far beyond Foucault's own philosophy. These three are: (1) that domains of objects are constituted by discourse; (2) that subjectivity itself is constituted; and (3) that the concepts of one time and one history need to be rejected. Thinking on these three theses will lead me to conclude this essay with some thoughts on Foucault on "transcendental philosophy."

It is interesting to notice that of these three theses, (1) is clearly one that is in the spirit of transcendental philosophy. (2) is also a thesis that, under a certain construal, is acceptable to the transcendental philosopher. (3) runs counter to a dominant trend in transcendental philosophy. These remarks bear out that all the three theses are closely related to Foucault's continuing concern with—though by no means acceptance of—transcendental philosophy.

1. The thesis of the *Archaeology* is well known: for each discourse there is no preexistent theme, such as madness, which that discourse simply takes up. On the contrary, it is "the interplay of rules that makes possible the appearance of objects during a given period of time."[16] It is discourse which constitutes a domain of objects. As some have noted, what needs to be demystified, according to Foucault, is the category of the "real," in the sense of an ontological category of reality behind and prior to discourse.[17] In a later essay, Foucault writes: "I wanted to see how these problems of constitution could be resolved within a historical framework, instead of referring them to a constituent object (madness, criminality or whatever)."[18] Phenomenology, especially French, solved it by historicizing the subject. Foucault wants to get rid of the subject—be it a transcendent, ahistorical ego ("an empty sameness throughout the course of history"), or a historicized principle and the constituting source. As we shall see, the subject itself is historically constituted. But what then is the principle of constitution? Not, to be sure, history in the familiar, let us say, traditional sense, for the idea of one, continuous, historical process unfolding itself in one time, is itself a construction, behind which stands the idea of a transcendental subject. With the pregiven object and the pregiven subject both out, constitution is by rules of discourse. But this structuralist theory is soon replaced by the socalled genealogy: all constitution, be it of the subject, of forms of discourse, or of their object domains, is said to be by power.

In view of Foucault's continuing critique of transcendental philosophy and of all constitution theories that trace constitution back to subjectivity, it is understandable that readers would notice his opposition to that tradition. But one is likely to overlook the fact that what he wants to set aside is only one half of that tradition—namely, the priority accorded to subjectivity. The other half he retains, and this is the general theory of constitution. The idea of constitution has its original home in the

Kantian-Husserlian tradition. It is incompatible with the naive realism and naturalism that many read into Foucault. Foucault belongs rather to a different tradition, stripped of the primacy of subjectivity. Power still occupies the place vacated by subjectivity. Power in effect is the transcendental, as discourse was in the *Archaeology*. Given, however, the nature of the concept of power to which I have drawn attention earlier in this essay, the nature of Foucault's transcendental thinking is all the more impressive. What is noteworthy is that there is a certain "bad faith" about it. Foucault—granted that his local genealogies are viable stories—lays claim to a universalist thesis about *all* objects, all discourses,[19] all subjectivity, which makes him a universal intellectual, which he at the same time does not want to be.

2. The radicalization of Foucault's thinking is best illustrated in his attempt to show that subjectivity itself is constituted, so that it cannot be the source of constitution. One must be able to understand the precise nature of this thesis, before one attempts to question its viability. There is a philosophical outlook, shared by many different sorts of philosophers, according to which "consciousness," "subjectivity," "mental," and the "inner" do not stand for any reality, but are rather products of misconstruing/misunderstanding something—that something may be the grammar of one's language, the nature of one's knowledge of oneself, or self-ascription of features. Be that as it may, this is not the sort of thesis Foucault wants to uphold. His attitude toward the principle of subjectivity is far more sophisticated. He is not, to be sure, a behaviorist or a reductionist. Subjectivity is "a constructed entity," but not false or imaginary.[20]

First of all, it is very important to bear in mind that when Foucault rejects subjectivity and consciousness, he rejects them as explanatory concepts. As Garth Gillan puts it, the break with subjectivity is but its elimination as a metatheoretical concept, while the subject remains an important object in the field of history.[21] So he is not denying that there are real subjects acting within history. What he is rejecting is that there is a subject who constitutes history and can provide a principle of explanation of history. So the familiar objections to the effect that without subjectivity we could not have agency and a genuine concept of action—won't be relevant against Foucault.

In the second place, although Foucault holds that the individual is not a pregiven entity, but is constituted by relations of power,[22] this thesis about constitution of individuality is not quite the same as the thesis about constitution of subject. An important part of Foucault's critique of consciousness is not merely that it is constituted, but that consciousness is not all transparent. This is a point which many others—notably

Merleau-Ponty—had pressed against Sartre, who is generally regarded as representative of the view that consciousness is all transparent. In *The Order of Things*, Foucault wrote that "'the Other' is that which both escapes consciousness, yet is constitutive to it."[23] The human sciences have been trying to retrieve this other, and to make it known, as is best exemplified in psychoanalysis. Hegel knew this, although he hoped that in absolute knowledge all opacity would be eliminated, and all otherness overcome. Kant, in his thesis of the sense representations (imprinted upon the mind by an other) and Husserl in his thesis about the *hyle* also show awareness of this opacity within the heart of consciousness—both escaped the consequences of this recognition by restricting "consciousness" to the noetic acts which synthesize and confer meaning. In any case, this is not a criticism that the transcendental-philosophical tradition did not know how to deal with.

If by the subject is meant not merely consciousness but also self-consciousness, then, of all persons, Hegel saw most clearly that self-consciousness is constituted, and constituted by desire, conflict of desires, struggle for recognition, a life and death battle, and exercise of power over others, the subjugated. There is no doubt that Foucault owes much to this account, even if he rejects a theory of power as domination.

I think, an account of the constitution of subjectivity has to be non-reductionist; and the minimum condition that it has to satisfy is that in its account of the constitution of *the most basic form* of subjectivity, it should be non-circular. With these in mind, let us turn to Foucault's account of constitution as presented in the essay "The Subject and Power." He tells us that his goal is to give a history of the different modes by which human beings are made subjects in our culture. In thus posing the question, he obviously has a very restricted sense of being a subject. A subject is one who is subjected to something by control or dependence, and this sense of subjectivity has a close proximity to the idea of subjugation. Struggles against subjugation are said to be directed against forms of subjectivity and submission. This makes perfectly good sense: struggles of a colonized people for freedom, of minority groups against suppression, or the Palestinians on the West Bank for freedom—all are eo ipso struggles against a certain form of subjectivity in each case. This entails another side of subjectivity[24] in Foucault's restricted sense: if the subject is a subject insofar he/she is subjugated, controlled, dependent, his/her specific form of subjectivity is also a sense of identity, a self-knowledge that he/she carries.

Given this sense of "subject," Foucault goes on to distinguish between three modes of "objectification" (or rather "subjectification"): (a) There are modes of inquiry, such as grammar, philosophy, and linguistics, which focus upon, thematize, objectify the speaking subject and modes of enquiry such as economics which focus upon, thematize, objectify the productive subject. (b) The subject is also objectified in what Foucault calls "dividing practices"—practices which divide men into binary oppositions mad/sane, sick/healthy, criminal/good boys. (c) Thirdly, human being may transform himself/herself into a subject by recognizing himself/herself as a subject of sexuality.

With regard to the first mode of objectification, I must say that it does not satisfy the requirement regarding noncircularity. Even leaving aside the muddle about an *objectification* as constituting *subjectivity* (this is precisely what, Husserl complains, distorts the true nature of subjectivity), it seems to me so clear that scientific thematization of a speaking or producing subject already presupposes prescientific subjectivity. How is the prescientific subjectivity constituted? My suspicion is that Foucault is not concerned with this question, he is concerned with, as stated earlier in this chapter, expelling the subject from a metatheoretical role, while leaving it its natural role in prescientific and first-level theories (histories, for example). But this should not give him the satisfaction that he has gotten rid of the constituting subjectivity. Leaving aside the question of what forms of subjective acts go into scientific thematization, we cannot avoid the role of subjectivity in constituting the prescientific world of the speaking and the producing subject.

What Foucault shows is how subjectivity is objectified. Another way of objectification—besides scientific thematization—is dividing it up as either mad or sane, sick or healthy, good or bad. But that this second mode of objectification ends up by distorting the nature subjectivity is precisely what Husserl and Sartre had insisted upon. So even if Foucault is right, what he regards as a step in the constitution of subjectivity works precisely in the opposite direction—it is a step toward covering up of subjectivity.

The third mode of objectification is clearly one of subjugation—subjugation, e.g., to sexuality. That is why Foucault could regard the subject as an inscription on the fractured body. The asylum, the confessional, the prison, and sexuality *subject* the body to discipline, inscribe power on it, make it self-conscious—thereby giving rise to modern subjectivity, and, on Foucault's theory, power is not a manifestation of consciousness. I suspect Foucault's *philosophical* thesis, not his historical result, confuses between subjectivity and its distorted forms. Hegel knew better. Foucault holds that the subject is constituted by power, and yet he also holds that power is exercised only over free subjects and only insofar as they are free.[25] There is a dimension of subjectivity underlying power, and "we have to promote new forms of subjectivity through the refusal of this kind of individuality."[26]

3. Finally, I consider the famed thesis about discontinuities and breaks, originally devised (by Bachelard) as a barrier against the claim of subjectivity to reflectively appropriate all history into its own being. Some time ago, I argued—against Foucault's thesis about epistemological breaks—that there is no nonarbitrary way of coming up with a series of discontinuous epochs, that if one chose a different leading clue (*Leitfaden*), one could have the ruptures fall at different places (or times).[27] Now I realize that is not contrary to Foucault's own intentions. Reflecting, at one place, on the thesis as presented in *The Order of Things*, Foucault writes: "for me, the whole business of breaks and non-breaks is always at once a point of departure and a very relative thing"—it may well mean "relative to the field of one's enquiry." We can shift the scenery, he goes on to say, and take as a starting point something else, change the reference points, and come up with a different story. Does the result depend on the choice of reference, and the choice of reference on one's conjecture?

These considerations suggest that my earlier objection does not effectively work against Foucault's position, for Foucault's position amounts to rejecting not only a monolithic "total" history, a continuous "grand narrative," but also a monolithic discontinuous narrative. The radical consequence of this thesis is that there is no one history, be it continuous or discontinuous, and no one time. Two things are happening at the same time: on the one hand, contrary to a dominant trend of modern philosophy from Kant onwards, Foucault wants to devalue time—even at the cost of seeming to spatialize time.[28] But the real reason underlying this devaluation of time is the realization that there are *times* rather than Time, that the many layers of social formation have their own times,[29] that the concepts of history and historicity themselves are of historical origin (what is the sense of this last occurrence of "historical"?). I believe, in this respect, Foucault's message is a welcome breath of fresh air in the midst of reigning historicisms. "History" and "Time" are themselves constituted out of histories and times. Whether this last thesis eliminates the need for a transcendental turn, or signals the possibility of a different sort of transcendental-constitutive theory, is a question I cannot respond to on this occasion. But one thing seems to me to be clear. One does not understand Foucault unless one understands the nature of his continuing concern with transcendental philosophy.

9

Phenomenology: Between Essentialism and Transcendental Philosophy

Phenomenology is caught between the extremes of an essentialistic realism and a transcendental constitution theory which looks like a form of *Bewusstseinsidealismus*. Essentialism holds that things have their essences, and that essences are a kind of entities *sui generis*. It further holds that truths about individual realities, contingent as they are, presuppose the necessary truths about the essences those realities instantiate or embody. If this be so, then a philosophy which aims at being a system of such essential truths about the various regions of being can at least hope to be able to provide the apodictic foundational framework that is presupposed by all empirical cognition. It is not as though such essential truths are merely ideals that the philosopher pursues like a will-o'-the-wisp. To the contrary, many such eidetic truths already are in our possession. Pure geometry and pure number theory are to be counted amongst them. Others are becoming amongst common acquisitions of philosophical common sense: that all conscious experiences are intentional; that all outer perceptions are perspectival; that all human existence is being-toward-death; that religious experience is characterized by an awareness of the sacred; or that a fictional character must necessarily lack full determinateness. These are not empirical, inductive generalizations, but rather essential truths arrived at after a process of imaginative variation.

Essentialism, however, has always aroused in philosophers a certain breed of deep suspicion. The philosophers I have in mind, when I say this, are not empiricists and nominalists. They can be easily refuted. But there are others who are so impressed by the open-endedness of the course of experience as well as of scientific research, who are also so impressed by the historicity of all truths and the process character of all things and the fallibility of all cognition, that they find in essentialism the opposite of everything they stand for. Essentialism arrests change, solidifies process, closes forever the possibility of revising the truths of the present—and ends up by making the real world, human experience, and scientific cognition rest on, and within the constraints of, an inviolable grid of unchangeable truths. What if we do not welcome such a prospect?

Freed from essentialism, transcendental constitution theory would appear to be able to reconcile itself with all that the anti-essentialist wants (save his realism, if he is a realist). The constitution theory need not be tied to a Kantian type of a priorism, with its fixed grid of a categorial framework. It can be a historicist theory, according to which the constitution of reality is a historical process of unfolding experience and thinking. If the constituted world forms a settled basis for future worldmaking, the already achieved leaves room for an open-endedness of the yet-to-come for, given the ideas of change, process, and contingency, who can predict what theories and thoughts will emerge, reshaping the world and its structure?

So far, it is good enough. But from where did the anti-essentialist philosopher derive his insight that reality and human existence and cognition are incurably historical, process-ridden, totally contingent and open-ended? Is this fundamental position borne out by experience? Or is it self-evidently true? Or is it the inevitable consequence of the contemporary *cultural* breakdown of essentialism? Or is it a consequence of the undeniable temporality of all things? Or is it borne out by any or all of the sciences to date?

Unfortunately for the philosopher of radical contingency, none of the alternatives is of any help. They are either self-defeating (for, if experience hitherto has borne this out, its radical contingency may well be rejected in the future by virtue of that very contingency), or begging the issue (for, it may just be that essentialism has not broken down, it is only taken to have broken down), or self-contradictory (for one may be unknowingly hypostatizing just one's favorite historicism or temporality or process-character into an irremediable essential structure), or just false (sciences do not teach a theory of radical change, but of change within a structure, mathematical or morphological; and it is arguable that not all things are temporal and, moreover, that temporality does not mean radical contingency, for temporality itself has an abiding structure, and experience bears witness to both change and permanence of forms, structures, types, and patterns, even of the simplest qualia).

What I am leading up to is the fact that essentialism need not be thrown out on grounds of one's favored metaphysical position. The task is to combine essentialism with change, history and open-endedness, and set aside that meaningless picture of radical contingency, according to which just everything is possible next instant.

Amongst philosophers of contingency, Merleau-Ponty recognizes the role of essences, even if that role is provisional. Amongst philosophers of process, Whitehead recognizes the role of "eternal objects" as making change intelligible. Amongst historicist philosophers, Marx and Marxists (such as Adorno) have recognized that without essences, in a purely nominalistic ontology, history would have no structure. In the heart of temporality, and of the flux-character of consciousness, Husserl discovered an abiding character: the form of the living present.

So let us not despair of the possibility of keeping together essentialism and transcendental philosophy. As a matter of fact, each of these would make up for the other's deficiency.

Let us at this point recall, from the earlier chapters, what has happened to the essences themselves. You may construe the essence either as a hidden metaphysical structure to be posited by thought but not graspable within experience, or as a theoretical entity posited within a scientific theory, or as an experienced, experiencable and so phenomenologically validated entity. The first is the Platonic essence, the second is the Kripkean essence (the essence of water is H_2O, if the theory eventually holds up), the last is the phenomenological essence, the entire or part of the *what* of the real individual, as abstracted from its instantiations or embodiments in real existence, and as determined to be invariant amidst imaginative variations. Such a phenomenal essence, determining or rather prescribing a rule of synthesis of possible experiences, in order that a concept may be validly applied, is not an ontological mystery, but an *eidos* in the strict sense, the visible form. It is grasped first unreflectively in everyday experience, then reflectively isolated and fixed.

A theory of constitution without essentialism has to start with bare particulars which did not exemplify or embody types. The resulting theory of constitution, I am afraid, would be phenomenalism, a form of psychological reductionism. For the anti-essentialist, conscious life also would be a flux of bare particulars. The recognition of essential structures on both sides—in the world and in consciousness—yields the prospect of a theory, an account not of how this this-there appears in this bit of experiential event, but of how things *such as* this are presented in experiences *such as* this. Essences thus give the inquiry a direction, a structure, and so a philosophical promise.

What Is Constitution?

With these introductory remarks intended to defend essentialism for my present limited purposes, let us ask: What does the talk of "constitution" really amount to? Note that since Husserl introduced it, it has come to be a part of the jargon of continental philosophy—even with radical anti-Husserlians. As we have seen, Foucault holds that the different social sciences just did not start by applying themselves to preexistent subject matter, as though madness was already there before psychiatry and penal institutions and forms of discourse developed, but rather that it is the disciplines and the forms of discourse which *constituted* the entity called "madness." When he made his much misunderstood and much maligned remark that man is the last to appear and would be the first to disappear from the scene—what he meant was that the subject matter called "man" was after all constituted by the rise of the human sciences in the last two centuries, and that theme would be dissolved when the human sciences are dissolved.

The first thing to realize, then, is that constitution, for Husserl (as also for Foucault) is not creation (contrary to Ingarden's reading of Husserl). Gaston Berger reports how much Husserl disapproved all talk of creation in this context. Note that all constitution is not active constitution (as is the case with cultural objectivities). In the case of the perceived world, constitution is passive.

Secondly, constitution analysis must follow the *Leitfaden* of the constituted sense, and no constitution analysis is strictly phenomenological if it is in conflict with the constituted sense. It belongs to the sense of the real world that the world exists in itself, no matter if it is perceived or not. This sense must be recovered within a constitution theory. How is the sense "*Ansichsein*" constituted?

Third, all constitution is constitution of sense, not of thing. Creation, on the other hand, is creation of things. Amongst the senses or component senses that ask for constitution analysis are senses such as "existence."

To give the constitution of a concept $\emptyset$ is to give those types of intentional experiences in which an object of the type $\emptyset$ is originally presented as a $\emptyset$. Thus, a physical object is originarily presented in outer perception—not in one snapshot, as it were, but in a sequentially unfolding manifold of them, not in visual perceptions alone, but also in tactual and actional ones, the manifold being subject to some appropriate sort of lawfulness.

Recall the following essential structure of intentional acts:

act ⟶ Noema or sense ⟶ object ⟶ fulfilling sense

The constitution of the object is to be explicated in two stages: (1) constitution of a noematic sense, and (2) constitution of the object through overlapping of noemata. The essence is grasped through ideation, i.e., through imaginative variations that let the boundaries of possible variations compatible with the thing's instantiating the essence stand out. The sense of the identity of a thing comes to relief through the overlapping of the various noemata through which that object is referred to.

Essentialism and a theory of ideal meanings thus are sound stepping-stones for transcendental constitution theory. It may appear, however, as though once you are at the level of constitution analysis, you are dealing with experiences, with the immanent stream of experiences, in the long run, of inner time-consciousness, and so one does not any longer need essences, since one is concerned with what one may call one's own transcendental experience. While this is indeed true, in-so-far as the reflecting phenomenologist has to see for himself how in one's ownmost experiences (now called "transcendental," inasmuch as one is thinking, and intuiting, within the most radical epoché) the transcendent objects are constituted, phenomenology as philosophy is not simply seeing, not simply "autobiography," but must lay down general truths about constitution, truths of the sort formulated above. In that case, the intuitive seeing in one's own case shall serve as an example for establishing essential laws of constitution. We shall then be back in an eidectic science. Thus, there would be, and we find this in Husserl's own thinking up to the end, a moving to and fro between a transcendental "empiriography" and an eidectics of transcendental life.

A Concluding Note

Let us briefly return to the baffling enigma: the relation between the empirical (subjectivity, ego) and the transcendental (subjectivity, the ego) It has been noted earlier that Husserl, in different contexts, speaks of their difference, identity, and parallelism. What then is the truth? Is it possible to combine these into one integral locution?

In the history of Indian philosophy, especially of the Vedanta, the relation between the empirical individual (*jiva*) and the universal Self (*Atman, Brahman*) has been variously conceived. Some took them to be different. In between these two extremes, we find an array of conceptualizations: "identity and difference," "identity in difference," "unthinkable (*acintya*) identity and difference," and even "utter inconceivability." The differences in the intellectual context notwithstanding, there is a striking affinity in the problematic. Now to turn to transcendental phenomenology.

To begin with, it is important to remember that the two *concepts* imply each other. Only from the transcendental point of view, the characterization of a stratum of experience as "empirical" makes sense. Otherwise, that modifier would serve no purpose. The same holds good from the other side as well: the contrast with "empirical" is internal to the idea of the transcendental.

Second, it is also necessary to get rid of the connection of "transcendental" to the "transcendent." The Platonic two-world theory dies hard, and once the two are separated, any attempt to put them together is destined to fail.

Third, the search for a common generic notion—e.g., of "life" in general—of which empirical life and transcendental life are specifications, is already on the wrong track.

We have only one stratum of experience, of consciousness, of life. To consider it as "empirical" is to interpret it as a part of nature, as subject to causal connections, as belonging to a psychophysical organism, as occurring in the objective time-series, and so forth. The same conscious experiences—perceptions, imaginations, thoughts—as meaning-bestowing, and so as having their respective noemata, and through them as constituting their objects, and through their horizonal characters constituting the worldliness of the world, through their idealizations constituting nature as a totality of objects into which that consciousness itself is then inserted—in brief, as the source of constitution, are transcendental.

Shall we then not say that it is transcendental subjectivity (and ego) which apperceives itself (recall Husserl's expression "mundanizing apperception") as empirical, mundane, as Homo sapiens, human, brain function, etc.? We have also to say, at the same time, that without such mundanizing self-interpretation, the transcendental would not apperceive itself as transcendental. To so apperceive itself is not to commit mistakes, to be under the spell of a metaphysical illusion. The metaphysical error is to reify the empirical as the transcendental, i.e., to simply identify them by ascribing the constituting function to the empirical (resulting in empirical idealism, psychologism, and such philosophical mistakes).

The empirical then is not a corruption in the being of the transcendental. It is in truth transcendental, it is also in truth a self—understanding on the part of the transcendental. Every feature of the empirical—corporeality, historicity, linguisticality—are preserved in the transcendental, only, as Husserl would say, "within quotation marks." To have discovered the sensory *hyle*, the kinaesthetic, the sign, the absent, within the transcendental is not to find what should not have been there. What is mistaken is the initial reading—not Husserl's, to be sure—that the transcendental is something else than what in fact it is—i.e., that is pure in some "theological" sense, uncorrupted, incorporeal, constantly self-present compressed into an instant, etc.

Notes

Chapter 1

1. For this, see J. N. Mohanty, "The Development of Husserl's Thought," in *A Companion to Husserl*, ed. Barry Smith and David Smith (New York: Cambridge University Press, 1995).
2. Cf. E. Husserl, *Ideas: General Introduction to Pure Phenomenology*, trans. W. Boyce Gibson (New York: McMillan, 1931) (henceforth referred to as *Ideas* I).
3. For a classic account of this, see A. Gurwitsch, "The Kantian and Husserlian Conceptions of Consciousness," in his *Studies in Phenomenology and Psychology* (Evanston: Northwestern University Press, 1966).
4. E. Husserl, *The Crisis of European Sciences and Transcendental Phenomenology*, trans. D. Carr (Evanston: Northwestern University Press, 1970).
5. Husserl, *Ideas* I, introduction.
6. This is worked out in ibid., chap. 1.
7. Ibid., § 2.
8. Ibid., § 15.
9. See J. N. Mohanty, *Transcendental Phenomenology: An Analytical Account* (Oxford: Blackwell, 1989).
10. Husserl, *Ideas* I, 22.
11. Ibid., § 3.

Chapter 2

1. F. H. Bradley, *The Principles of Logic*, vol. 1 (Oxford: Clarendon Press, 1958), 5–7.
2. M. Scheler, *Selected Philosophical Essays*, trans. D. Lachterman (Evanston: Northwestern University Press, 1973), 292–93.
3. Cf. E. Husserl, *Logical Investigations*, vol. 2, trans. J. N. Findlay (New York: Humanities Press, 1970), 773–800.
4. Cf. J. Hessen, *Max Scheler* (Essen: Hans V. Chamier, 1948), 27–29.
5. On the need for "love," Scheler writes: "Ohne eine Tendenz in dem Seienden, das 'weiss,' aus sich hervor- und *herauszugehen* zur Teilhabe an einem anderen Seinden, gibt es überhaupt kein mögliches 'Wissen.' Ich sehe keinen anderen Namen fur diese Tendenz als *Liebe*, Hingebung: gleichsam Sprengung

der Grenzen des eigenen Seins und Soseins durch Liebe" ("Erkenntnis und Arbeit," in *Die Wissenformen und die Gesellschaft* [Bern and Munich: Francke Verlag, Zweite Auflage, 1960], 204).

 6. See Scheler, *Selected Philosophical Essays*, 202–87.
 7. E. Lask, *Die Logik der Philosophie und die Katergorienlehre* (Tübingen, 1911).
 8. Scheler, *Selected Philosophical Essays*, 203–4.
 9. M. Merleau-Ponty, *Phenomenology of Perception*, trans C. Smith (London: Routledge and Kegan Paul, 1962), 3–12.
 10. Scheler states his view about sensation in a paradoxical form: "Sie [Empfindung] bezeichnet ein X-Erlebnis, das wir nie haben, auch nie haben können, solange wir leben, das wir aber in dem Grenzfall hätten, wenn wir—'tot' wären; wobei das doch wiederum seltsam ist, da, wenn wir tot wären, wir sicher keinerlei 'Erlebnis' mehr hätten!" (*Die Wissensformen*, 323).
 11. Ibid., 343.
 12. Scheler, *Selected Philosophical Essays*, 235–36.
 13. In Scheler, *Die Wisensformen*. See n. 16.
 14. Ibid., 241.
 15. Ibid., 198.
 16. Scheler, *Selected Philosophical Essays*, 24.
 17. Ibid., 24, 157–58.
 18. Ibid., 158.
 19. Ibid.
 20. Husserl, *Ideas* I, § 4.
 21. Scheler, *Selected Philosophical Essays*, 222; see also *Die Wissensformen*, 310–11.
 22. Scheler, *Selected Philosophical Essays*, 315.
 23. M. Scheler, *Späte Schriften* (Bern and Munich: Francke Verlag, 1976), 41.
 24. See J. Habermas, *Knowledge and Human Interests*, trans. Jeremy S. Shapiro (Boston: Beacon Press, 1971).
 25. Husserl, *Logische Untersuchungen*, vol. 2 (Halle: Max Niemeyer, 1928), part 1, 223.
 26. Cf. M. Merleau-Ponty, *The Primacy of Perception*, ed., trans. James M. Edie (Evanston: Northwestern University Press, 1964), 75–76.

Chapter 3

 1. Nicolai Hartmann, *Zur Grundlegung der Ontologie*, 4th ed. (Meisenheim am Glan: Anton Hein, 1948), 56.
 2. Ibid., 43.
 3. Nicolai Hartmann, *Grundzüge einer Metaphysik der Erkenntnis*, 4th ed. (Berlin: Walter Gruyter, 1949), 508.
 4. Nicolai Hartmann, *Möglichkeit und Wirklichkeit*, 2d ed. (Meisenheim am Glan: Anton Hein, 1979).
 5. Cf. Joseph König, "Über einen neuen Beweis des Satzes von der Notwendigkeit alles Geschehens," *Archiv für Philiosophie* (1948), 5–43.

6. I have developed further criticisms of Hartmann's modal theory in J. N. Mohanty, *Phenomenology and Ontology* (The Hague: Nijhoff, 1970).

Chapter 4

1. Roman Ingarden, *Des Literarische Kunstwerk* (Tübingen: Max Niemeyer, 1965); *The Literary Work of Art*, trans. G. Grabowicz (Evanston: Northwestern University Press, 1973).
2. Ingarden, *Der Streit um die Existenz der Welt*, 3 vols. (Tübingen: Niemeyer, 1964–74).
3. Ingarden, *The Literary Work of Art*, § 20.
4. Ibid., 126.
5. Ibid., 221.
6. R. Ingarden, "Aesthetic Experience and Aesthetic Object," *Philosophy and Phenomenological Research* (March 1961), 311.
7. R. Ingarden, "Artistic and Aesthetic Values," *British Journal of Aesthetics* 4 (1964), 200.
8. Ibid., 202.
9. Published in *Analecta Husserliana*, vol. 2, 357–74.
10. Ibid., 367–68.
11. "Letter to Ed. Husserl" (1918), *Analecta Husserliana*, vol. 2, 361.
12. See R. Ingarden, *On the Motives which led Husserl to Transcendental Idealism* (The Hague: Nijhoff, 1975), 12.
13. Ibid., 25.
14. I. Kant, *Critique of Pure Reason*, trans. N. K. Smith (New York: St. Martin's, 1965), A104.
15. Ingarden, *On the Motives*, 21.
16. Ibid., 25.
17. J. N. Mohanty, *The Possibility of Transcendental Philosophy* (The Hague: Kluwer, 1985).
18. R. Ingarden, "Probleme der Husserlschen Reduktion," *Analecta Husserliana* 4 (1976), 1–71, esp. 25.
19. Ibid., 40.
20. Husserl Archive Manuscript no. A V 5.
21. Husserl Archive Manuscript no. A VI 10.
22. Cf. A. Gurwitsch, *Field of Consciousness* (Pittsburgh: Duquesne University Press, 1964), 404ff.
23. A. Gurwitsch, *Studies in Phenomenology and Psychology* (Evanston: Northwestern University Press, 1966), 92.

Chapter 5

1. E. Husserl, *Ideas: General Introduction to Pure Phenomenology*, trans. W. Boyce Gibson (New York: MacMillan, 1931), § 36.

2. Ibid., § 7.
3. Ibid., § 15.
4. Ibid., § 36.
5. E. Husserl, *Phänomenologische Psychologie*, in *Husserliana*, vol. 9, 167.
6. E. Husserl, *Erfahrung und Urteil* (Hamburg: Claasen und Goverts, 1948), Beilage I, 460–71.

Chapter 6

1. See J. N. Mohanty, *The Concept of Intentionality* (St. Louis: Warren Green, 1972).
2. See J. N. Mohanty, *The Possibility of Transcendental Philosophy* (The Hague: Kluwer, 1985).
3. I am here referring to two of Carr's unpublished papers.
4. See Mohanty, *The Possibility of Transcendental Philosophy*.
5. Frank Kirkland has suggested this line of relating Kant to Husserl in some of his papers.

Chapter 7

1. J. Derrida, *Speech and Phenomena*, trans. David Allison (Evanston: Northwestern University Press, 1973), 88.
2. J. Derrida, *Margins of Philosophy*, trans. Alan Bass (Chicago: University of Chicago Press, 1982), 158.
3. Cf. J. Caputo, "The Economy of Signs in Husserl and Derrida: From Uselessness to Full Employment," in *Deconstruction and Philosophy: The Texts of Jacques Derrida*, ed. John Sallis (Chicago: University of Chicago Press, 1987), 99–113, esp. 100–101.
4. Cf. Caputo, ibid., 104–5.
5. This review appeared in *Les études philosophiques* (1965), 617–19.
6. Derrida, *Speech and Phenomena*, 82.
7. Cf. P. Ricoeur, *Husserl: An Analysis of His Phenomenology*, trans. E. Ballard and L. Embree (Evanston: Northwestern University Press, 1967), esp. 29–30.
8. Derrida, *Speech and Phenomena*, 34.
9. Ricoeur also suggests this translation. See his *Husserl*, 216.
10. Derrida, *Speech and Phenomena*, 35.
11. Derrida, *Margins*, 117.
12. Ibid., 118. However, in a later context, Derrida appears to be saying "Er [Husserl] warf Heidegger—*zu Recht, wie ich glaube*—vor, die Phänomenologie anthropologisiert zu haben" (In Benedikt, Michael and Berger, Rudolf, eds, *Die Krise der Phänomenologie und die Pragmatik des Wissenschaftsfortschritts*, ed. M. Benedikt and R. Berger [Vienna: Österreische Staatsdruckerei, 1986], 177; my italics).
13. Cf. my comments on this text in J. N. Mohanty, "Consciousness and Existence: Remarks on the Relation between Husserl and Heidegger," *Man and*

World 2 (1978), 324–35; reprinted in J. N. Mohanty, *The Possibility of Transcendental Philosophy* (The Hague: Nijhoff, 1985), 155–65.
   14. E. Husserl, *Logical Investigations*, vol. 1, trans. J. N. Findlay (New York: Humanities Press, 1970), Investigation 1, § 15.
   15. J. Derrida, *Limited Inc* (Evanston: Northwestern University Press, 1988), 58.
   16. M. Merleau-Ponty, *Phenomenology of Perception*, trans. C. Smith (London: Routledge and Kegan Paul, 1962), 71.
   17. Derrida, *Limited Inc*, 116.
   18. Derrida, *Speech and Phenomena*, 52.
   19. Ibid., 53.
   20. Derrida, *Limited Inc*, 77.
   21. Ibid., 60.
   22. Ibid., 79.
   23. Ibid., 136.
   24. J. Derrida, *Husserls Weg in die Geschichte am Leitfaden der Geometrie*, trans. R. Hentschel and A. Knop (Munich: Wilhelm Fink Verlag, 1987).
   25. E. Husserl, *Philosophie der Arithmetik* (*Husserliana*, vol. 12), 241 fn.
   26. *The Crisis of European Sciences and Transcendental Phenomenology*, trans. D. Carr (Evanston: Northwestern University Press, 1970), 358.
   27. Ibid., 360–61.
   28. Ibid., 361.
   29. Derrida, *Husserls Weg*, 183.
   30. Husserl, *Logical Investigations*, vol. 1, 23.
   31. Derrida, *Speech and Phenomena*, 43.
   32. Husserl, *Philosophie der Arithmetik*, 243.
   33. David Wood recognizes this. See his *An Introduction to Derrida* (Thetford: The Thetford Press, 1985).
   34. Derrida, *Speech and Phenomena*, 55.
   35. Derrida, "Genesis und Struktur in die Phänomenologie," in *Die Schrift und die Differenz*, trans. R. Gash (Frankfurt: Suhrkamp, 1972), esp. 243.
   36. Thus, e.g., Husserl writes: "Die Tatsachen, die der Historizismus geltend macht, brauchen wir demnach nicht erst in irgenwelche Krittischen Erwägungen zu ziehen" (*Krisis*, in *Husserliana*, vol. 6, 383).
   37. "Dabei haben wir uns jeder Bindung an die faktisch geltende historische Welt enthoben . . ." (Ibid.).
   38. Ibid., 380.
   39. Ibid., 386.
   40. Derrida, *Husserls Weg*, 126.
   41. Ibid., 135.
   42. Ibid., 145–46, 161–62, 192 fn.
   43. Ibid., 193 fn., 192.
   44. E. Ströker, *Husserl's Transcendental Phenomenology*, trans. L. Hardy (Stanford: Stanford University Press, 1993).
   45. Ibid., 182 fn.

46. Ibid., 183.
47. Ibid., 184.
48. Ibid.
49. This distinction between transcendent fact and transcendental fact is nicely made by Karl-Heinz Lembeck in his *Gegenstand Geschichte: Geschichtswissenschaftstheorie in Husserls Phänomenologie* (Dordrecht: Kluwer, 1988), see esp. chap. 6.
50. E. Husserl, *Cartesian Meditations*, trans. D. Cairns (The Hague: Nijhoff, 1960), § 64.
51. J. Derrida, "Antwort an Apel," *Zeitmitschrift für Aesthetik* (Summer 1987), 79.
52. Ibid., 83.

Chapter 8

1. M. Foucault, *Power/Knowledge: Selected Interviews and Other Writings, 1972–1977*, ed. C. Gordon (New York: Pantheon Books, 1980), 165.
2. Ibid., 65.
3. Ibid., 81.
4. Ibid., 103.
5. Ibid., 66.
6. Ibid., 89.
7. Ibid., 73–74.
8. Ibid., 98.
9. Ibid., 131.
10. Ibid., 141–42.
11. M. Foucault, *The History of Sexuality*, vol. 2, trans. R. Heedly (New York: Vintage, 1980), 86.
12. G. W. F. Hegel, *Phenomenology of Mind*, trans. J. B. Baillie (London and New York: Humanities Press, 1966), 132.
13. M. Foucault, "The Discourse of Language," trans. Rupert Sawyer, printed as an appendix to *The Archaeology of Knowledge* (New York: Random House, 1972).
14. David Hoy defends such an interpretation in his "Genealogy versus Rational Reconstruction: Two Conflicting Conceptions of How to Naturalize Philosophy," read at a Temple University conference in September 1987.
15. M. Foucault, "The Subject and Power," *Critical Inquiry* 8 (1982), 777–95, esp. 778.
16. Foucault, *The Archaeology of Knowledge*, 15.
17. Mark Cousins and Athar Hussain, *Michael Foucault* (New York: MacMillan, 1984), 261.
18. Foucault, *Power/Knowledge*, 117.
19. Foucault recognizes that his general thesis regarding medicine and psychiatric practice is difficult to extend to theoretical physics and organic chemistry. See ibid., 109.
20. Ibid., 239.

21. C. Lemert and G. Gillan, *Michel Foucault: Social Theory as Transgression* (New York: Columbia University Press, 1982), 101.

22. Foucault, *Power/Knowledge*, 74.

23. M. Foucault, *The Order of Things: An Archaeology of the Human Sciences* (New York: Random House, 1970), 322.

24. Foucault, "The Subject of Power," 786.

25. Ibid., 790.

26. Ibid., 785.

27. J. N. Mohanty, *Transcendental Phenomenology: An Analytic Account* (Oxford: Blackwell, 1989), 119–21.

28. Foucault, *Power/Knowledge*, 70, 149–50.

29. Foucault, *The Archaeology of Knowledge*, 131.

Index

Absence, 12
Adorno, 90
Aesthetic object, 35–6
Anthropologism, 65–66
Aristotle, 30
Art, 32, 34, 35

Bachelard, G., 87
Berger, G., 63, 91
Bradley, F.H., 15, 95
Brentano, F., 42, 47, 64

Caputo, J., 98
Carnap, R., 7
Carr, D., 5, 6, 58, 98, 99
Cohen, H., 25, 61
Concretum, 7, 48
Consciousness, 2, 3, 8, 10, 12, 30, 34, 36, 37, 38, 39, 41–42, 43, 44, 45, 47, 48, 52, 55, 67, 81, 84, 85, 88, 93
Constitution, 8, 10, 12, 34, 37, 38, 43, 53, 54, 63, 67, 69, 71–72, 75, 79, 83–85, 88–89, 90–93
Context, 66–8
Croce, B., 81

Death, 66–67
Deconstruction, 62, 68, 75, 76
Derrida, J., 61, ch. 7, 98, 99, 100
Dewaehlens, 63
Dewey, J., 20
Difference, 67, 92
Dilthey, W., 14, 22, 69
Discontinuity, 81, 79, 87
Discourse, 79, 83, 84

Ego, 40, 42, 67; transcendental, 10, 26, 53, 63, 83, 92, 93

Eidetic Singularity, 5–6
Existence, 7, 9, 14, 21, 22, 23, 26, 27, 44, 45, 48, 49, 54, 90, 91
Experience, transcendental, 92

Fact, transcendental, 74, 75, 100
Fictional objects, 35
Findlay, J.N., 81
Fink, E., 57
Føllesdal, D., 47, 64
Foucault, ch. 8, 91, 100
Frege, G., 64
Freud, S., 61

Gautama, 22
Gehlen, A., 23
Geist, 15, 22, 27, 81–87
Genealogy, 82, 83, 84
Genesis, 72–73
Gillan, G., 84
Gurwitsch, A., 19, 95, 97

Habermas, J., 23
Hartmann, N., 9, 14, 22, ch. 3, 96, 97
Hegel, G.F., 22, 54, 57, 61, 63, 65, 79, 81, 85, 100
Heidegger, M., 15, 22, 26, 59, 63, 64, 65, 66, 79, 98
Hessen, J., 95
Hintikka, J., 64
Historicism, xi, xii, 12, 13, 73, 74, 87, 89, 90, 99
History, 12, 13, 54, 69, 73, 74–75, 77, 78, 79, 83, 84, 85, 86, 87, 90
Hoy, D., 100
Hyppolite, J., 63, 82

103

INDEX

Idealism, 14, 22, 32, 33, 36, 37, 41, 42, 43, 63, 64
Identity, 67, 68, 92
Indication, 68, 70
Individual, 7, 48
Ingarden, R., 9, 10, 20, ch. 4, 91, 97
Intentional act, 1, 8, 9, 30, 33, 37, 42, 44, 53, 67, 91
Intentional object, 33–34
Intentionality, 32, 33, 34, 47, 49, 50, 53, 57, 60, 61, 63, 65, 66, 67, 72
Intimation, 68, 70
Intuition, xi, 11, 12, 15, 16, 18, 20, 21, 23, 39, 54, 63, 71, 72

James, W., 20
Jung, G., 61

Kant, I., xi, xii, 5, 7, 37, 42, 45, 52, 53, 54, 55, 56, 58, 59, 61, 74, 84, 85, 87, 89, 95
Kirkland, F., 98
Knowledge, 14, 15, 16, 17, 18, 19, 20, 21, 22, 23, 25–26, 29–30, 31
Kojeve, A., 63, 65
Köning, J., 96

Landgrebe, L., 57
Lask, E., 96
Leibniz, 27, 28, 29
Lembeck, K.H., 100
Levinas, E., 63
Life-world, 1, 2, 3, 12, 13, ch. 6, 64
Living present, 12, 67

Marx, K., 63, 90
Meaning, 1, 2, 7–8, 13, 33–34, 36, 38, 42, 46, 54–55, 56, 61, 63, 64, 66, 67, 68, 69, 70, 71, 73, 92, 93
Meinong, A., 25, 40
Merleau-Ponty, M., 15, 23, 61, 63, 65, 67, 72, 79, 85, 90, 96, 99
Metaphysics, 12, 73, 74–75
Modality, 26, 27
Monologue, 68, 69
Müller, G., 81

Natorp, P., 25, 64
Naturalism, 3
Necessity, 4, 28, 29, 88
Nelson, 37

Neo-Kantianism, 22, 25, 64
Noema, 1, 2, 8, 10, 30, 33, 36, 37, 38, 42, 45, ch. 5, 61, 67, 70, 71, 92
Noesis, 2, 42, 45, 46, 61

Objectification, 85, 86
Ontology, 25, 26, 41, 46

Peirce, 20
Perception, 17, 18, 19, 38, 45, 59
Pfänder, A., 9
Physicalism, 57–58
Plato, 11, 64
Plessner, H., 23
Possibility, 28, 29, 71
Power, 79, 80, 81, 82, 83, 84, 85, 86
Pragmatism, 20, 23
Presence, 72
Principle of Individuation, 6–7
Psychologism, 3, 64, 93

Realism, 22, 30, 31, 33, 39, 43, 63, 64, 84; critical, 14, 15
Reality, 21, 22, 27, 28, 29, 30, 31, 32, 34, 36, 37, 40, 45, 46
Reason, 73, 82
Reduction, 9, 10, 11, 37, 38, 40, 41, 42, 43, 44, 50, 65, 68; eidetic, 9, 10, 21, 23, 26, 39, 49; phenomenological, 9, 10, 56; transcendental, 10, 21, 40, 57, 63, 65, 70, 88
Ricoeur, P., 63, 64, 65, 98

Santayana, G., 22
Sartre, J.-P., 63, 79, 85, 86
Scheler, M., 9, ch. 2, 95, 96
Schiller, F.C.S., 20
Scotus, Dun, 39
Sign, 12, 68, 95
Sinn, 46, 61, 91
Smith, B., 65, 95
Smith, D., 95
Speech, 69, 70
Strauss, E., 15
Ströker, E., 99
Subjectivity, 84, 85, 86; transcendental, 1, 12–13, 22, 52, 55, 58, 59, 61, 63, 64, 66, 73, 74, 75, 79, 83, 87, 92, 93

Time, 35, 51, 63, 66, 74, 79, 87, 89

INDEX

Transcendence, 36, 44
Truth, 38, 39, 45, 79, 80, 81

Whitehead, A.N., 90

Wolff, C., 29
Wood, D., 99
Writing, 69, 70